Anne Hutchinson

D1308173

Anne Hutchinson

ELIZABETH ILGENFRITZ

90-115
LIBRARY
COLUMBUS SCHOOL FOR GIRLS

CHELSEA HOUSE PUBLISHERS

NEW YORK · PHILADELPHIA

B
Hutchinson

Chelsea House Publishers
EDITOR-IN-CHIEF Remmel Nunn
MANAGING EDITOR Karyn Gullen Browne
COPY CHIEF Juliann Barbato
PICTURE EDITOR Adrian G. Allen
ART DIRECTOR Maria Epes
DEPUTY COPY CHIEF Mark Rifkin
ASSISTANT ART DIRECTOR Noreen Romano
MANUFACTURING MANAGER Gerald Levine
SYSTEMS MANAGER Lindsey Ottman
PRODUCTION MANAGER Joseph Romano
PRODUCTION COORDINATOR Marie Claire Cebrián

American Women of Achievement
SENIOR EDITOR Kathy Kuhtz

Staff for ANNE HUTCHINSON
ASSOCIATE EDITOR Ellen Scordato
COPY EDITOR Joseph Roman
EDITORIAL ASSISTANT Leigh Hope Wood
PICTURE RESEARCHER Patricia Burns
DESIGNER Diana Blume
COVER ILLUSTRATOR Patti Oleon, from a painting by Edmund
Dulac; map courtesy Boston Athenaeum.

Copyright © 1991 by Chelsea House Publishers, a division of
Main Line Book Co. All rights reserved. Printed and bound in
the United States of America.

First Printing

1 3 5 7 9 8 6 4 2

Library of Congress Cataloging-in-Publication Data

IlgenFritz, Elizabeth.
   Anne Hutchinson/by Elizabeth IlgenFritz.
      p.   cm.—(American women of achievement)
   Includes bibliographical references.
   Summary: Recounts the story of the Puritan woman who
was banished from her colony for being outspoken against the
religious leaders there.
   ISBN 1-55546-660-5
         0-7910-0439-2 (pbk.)
   1. Hutchinson, Anne Marbury, 1591–1643—Juvenile
literature.   2. Puritans—Massachusetts—Biography—Juvenile
literature.   3. Massachusetts—History—Colonial period, ca.
1600–1775—Juvenile literature.   [1. Hutchinson, Anne Marbury, 1591–1643.   2. Puritans.]   I. Title.   II. Series.
F67.H92I54   1990
973.2'2'092—dc20   90-33748
[B]   CIP
[92]   AC

CONTENTS

AMERICAN WOMEN OF ACHIEVEMENT

Abigail Adams
women's rights advocate

Jane Addams
social worker

Louisa May Alcott
author

Marian Anderson
singer

Susan B. Anthony
woman suffragist

Ethel Barrymore
actress

Clara Barton
founder of the American Red Cross

Elizabeth Blackwell
physician

Nellie Bly
journalist

Margaret Bourke-White
photographer

Pearl Buck
author

Rachel Carson
biologist and author

Mary Cassatt
artist

Agnes de Mille
choreographer

Emily Dickinson
poet

Isadora Duncan
dancer

Amelia Earhart
aviator

Mary Baker Eddy
founder of the Christian Science church

Betty Friedan
feminist

Althea Gibson
tennis champion

Emma Goldman
political activist

Helen Hayes
actress

Lillian Hellman
playwright

Katharine Hepburn
actress

Karen Horney
psychoanalyst

Anne Hutchinson
religious leader

Mahalia Jackson
gospel singer

Helen Keller
humanitarian

Jeane Kirkpatrick
diplomat

Emma Lazarus
poet

Clare Boothe Luce
author and diplomat

Barbara McClintock
biologist

Margaret Mead
anthropologist

Edna St. Vincent Millay
poet

Julia Morgan
architect

Grandma Moses
painter

Louise Nevelson
sculptor

Sandra Day O'Connor
Supreme Court justice

Georgia O'Keeffe
painter

Eleanor Roosevelt
diplomat and humanitarian

Wilma Rudolph
champion athlete

Florence Sabin
medical researcher

Beverly Sills
opera singer

Gertrude Stein
author

Gloria Steinem
feminist

Harriet Beecher Stowe
author and abolitionist

Mae West
entertainer

Edith Wharton
author

Phillis Wheatley
poet

Babe Didrikson Zaharias
champion athlete

CHELSEA HOUSE PUBLISHERS

"REMEMBER THE LADIES"

MATINA S. HORNER

Remember the Ladies." That is what Abigail Adams wrote to her husband, John, then a delegate to the Continental Congress, as the Founding Fathers met in Philadelphia to form a new nation in March of 1776. "Be more generous and favorable to them than your ancestors. Do not put such unlimited power in the hands of the Husbands. If particular care and attention is not paid to the Ladies," Abigail Adams warned, "we are determined to foment a Rebellion, and will not hold ourselves bound by any Laws in which we have no voice, or Representation."

The words of Abigail Adams, one of the earliest American advocates of women's rights, were prophetic. Because when we have not "remembered the ladies," they have, by their words and deeds, reminded us so forcefully of the omission that we cannot fail to remember them. For the history of American women is as interesting and varied as the history of our nation as a whole. American women have played an integral part in founding, settling, and building our country. Some we remember as remarkable women who—against great odds—achieved distinction in the public arena: Anne Hutchinson, who in the 17th century became a charismatic religious leader; Phillis Wheatley, an 18th-century black slave who became a poet; Susan B. Anthony, whose name is synonymous with the 19th-century women's rights movement and who led the struggle to enfranchise women; and, in our own century, Amelia Earhart, the first woman to cross the Atlantic Ocean by air.

These extraordinary women certainly merit our admiration, but other women, "common women," many of them all but forgotten, should also be recognized for their contributions to American thought and culture. Women have been community builders; they have founded schools and formed voluntary associations to help those in need; they have assumed the major responsibility for rearing children, passing on from one generation to the next the values that keep a culture alive. These and innumerable other contributions, once ignored, are now being recognized by scholars, students, and the public. It is exciting and gratifying to realize that a part of our history that was hardly acknowledged a few generations ago is now being studied and brought to light.

In recent decades, the field of women's history has grown from obscurity to a politically controversial splinter movement to academic respectability, in many cases mainstreamed into such traditional disciplines as history, economics, and psychology. Scholars of women, both female and male, have organized research centers at such prestigious institutions as Wellesley College, Stanford University, and the University of California. Other notable centers for women's studies are the Center for the American Woman and Politics at the Eagleton Institute of Politics at Rutgers University; the Henry A. Murray Research Center for the Study of Lives, at Radcliffe College; and the Women's Research and Education Institute, the research arm of the Congressional Caucus on Women's Issues. Other scholars and public figures have established archives and libraries, such as the Schlesinger Library on the History of Women in America, at Radcliffe College, and the Sophia Smith Collection, at Smith College, to collect and preserve the written and tangible legacies of women.

From the initial donation of the Women's Rights Collection in 1943, the Schlesinger Library grew to encompass vast collections documenting the manifold accomplishments of American women. Simultaneously, the women's movement in general and the academic discipline of women's studies in particular also began with a narrow definition and gradually expanded their mandate. Early causes such as woman suffrage and social reform, abolition and organized labor were joined by newer concerns such as the history of women in business and the professions and in politics and government; the study of the family; and social issues such as health policy and education.

Women, as historian Arthur M. Schlesinger, jr., once pointed out, "have constituted the most spectacular casualty of traditional history.

They have made up at least half the human race, but you could never tell that by looking at the books historians write." The new breed of historians is remedying that omission. They have written books about immigrant women and about working-class women who struggled for survival in cities and about black women who met the challenges of life in rural areas. They are telling the stories of women who, despite the barriers of tradition and economics, became lawyers and doctors and public figures.

The women's studies movement has also led scholars to question traditional interpretations of their respective disciplines. For example, the study of war has traditionally been an exercise in military and political analysis, an examination of strategies planned and executed by men. But scholars of women's history have pointed out that wars have also been periods of tremendous change and even opportunity for women, because the very absence of men on the home front enabled them to expand their educational, economic, and professional activities and to assume leadership in their homes.

The early scholars of women's history showed a unique brand of courage in choosing to investigate new subjects and take new approaches to old ones. Often, like their subjects, they endured criticism and even ostracism by their academic colleagues. But their efforts have unquestionably been worthwhile, because with the publication of each new study and book another piece of the historical patchwork is sewn into place, revealing an increasingly comprehensive picture of the role of women in our rich and varied history.

Such books on groups of women are essential, but books that focus on the lives of individuals are equally indispensable. Biographies can be inspirational, offering their readers the example of people with vision who have looked outside themselves for their goals and have often struggled against great obstacles to achieve them. Marian Anderson, for instance, had to overcome racial bigotry in order to perfect her art and perform as a concert singer. Isadora Duncan defied the rules of classical dance to find true artistic freedom. Jane Addams had to break down society's notions of the proper role for women in order to create new social institutions, notably the settlement house. All of these women had to come to terms both with themselves and with the world in which they lived. Only then could they move ahead as pioneers in their chosen callings.

Biography can inspire not only by adulation but also by realism. It helps us to see not only the qualities in others that we hope to emulate but also, perhaps, the weaknesses that made them "human." By helping us identify with the subject on a more personal level they help us to feel that we, too, can achieve such goals. We read about Eleanor Roosevelt, for example, who occupied a unique and seemingly enviable position as the wife of the president. Yet we can sympathize with her inner dilemma: an inherently shy woman who had to force herself to live a most public life in order to use her position to benefit others. We may not be able to imagine ourselves having the immense poetic talent of Emily Dickinson, but from her story we can understand the challenges faced by a creative woman who was expected to fulfill many family responsibilities. And though few of us will ever reach the level of athletic accomplishment displayed by Wilma Rudolph or Babe Zaharias, we can still appreciate their spirit, their overwhelming will to excel.

A biography is a multifaceted lens. It is first of all a magnification, the intimate examination of one particular life. But at the same time, it is a wide-angle lens, informing us about the world in which the subject lived. We come away from reading about one life knowing more about the social, political, and economic fabric of the time. It is for this reason, perhaps, that the great New England essayist Ralph Waldo Emerson wrote, in 1841, "There is properly no history: only biography." And it is also why biography, and particularly women's biography, will continue to fascinate writers and readers alike.

Anne Hutchinson

On November 7, 1637, Anne Hutchinson defended herself at the
Massachusetts General Court before 49 ministers and magistrates. Her
trial was one of the first in American history to deal with the issue of
religious liberty.

ONE

"The Court Calls Mistress Anne Hutchinson"

On a bitterly cold November day in 1637, Anne Marbury Hutchinson began the arduous five-mile journey from her home in Boston to the church and meetinghouse in Newtown (present-day Cambridge). Beneath gray skies, over frozen paths slick with new-fallen snow, the pregnant, 46-year-old Hutchinson slowly made her way to the ferry that would bear her across the ice-clogged Charles River. Huddled in her cloak against the cold, stung by wind and spray, she contemplated her destination. In a plain square wooden building, Governor John Winthrop of the Massachusetts Bay Colony and dozens of magistrates and ministers were gathering for the November meeting of the Massachusetts General Court. Ordinarily, Hutchinson would not leave her comfortable home on such a dank and bone-chilling day to attend, but she had compelling cause for undertaking the unpleasant expedition. She was traveling to her own trial.

When Hutchinson finally arrived at the meetinghouse, spectators packed the chilly, ill-lit room, and still more were hurrying up the front steps. Few events in the eight-year history of the Massachusetts Bay Colony had stirred so much interest. The trial of this outspoken, educated, popular woman touched issues central to the founding of the colony itself and the life of each inhabitant. Chartered by King Charles I of England in 1629, Massachusetts Bay was a haven for devout reformers called Puritans who were distressed by the condition of the church and religious oppression in their homeland. John Winthrop, governor and founder of the colony, had brought Hutchinson to trial for troubling the peace of the small settlement. She had criticized prominent ministers and supported her brother-in-law the Reverend John Wheelwright in a dispute against other preachers. She welcomed her female neighbors, far from home and burdened with tasks in a rough new land, at popular weekly meetings in her home, where she discussed religion, the merits of sermons, and her understanding of theology.

Such activities would be innocuous in another time and place, but Massachusetts Bay was nearly a theocracy (a state in which religious leaders have governmental power). Although Puritans made sure that religious authorities did not hold formal political positions, they believed that religious beliefs informed every aspect of life in a God-fearing community. The secular (nonreligious) leaders were bound to protect the one true religion and to discipline any congregation or member who strayed from proper beliefs. Criticism of church leaders by Hutchinson and her followers equaled political rebellion in Winthrop's eyes, and he was determined to silence her and the Hutchinsonians.

Save for the foot warmers available to the magistrates presiding at the trial, the meetinghouse had no heat. Spectators and judges alike kept on their woolen gloves, no man removed his tall black hat, and each woman's bonnet was securely tied beneath her chin—all in a feeble attempt to ward off the icy drafts in the room. Governor John Winthrop, chief judge and prosecutor, sat at a table between former governor John Endecott and Deputy Governor Thomas Dudley. The court reporter, Simon Bradstreet, sat off to one side. On 3 long wooden benches behind Winthrop sat 9 magistrates, 31 deputies of the general court, and 8 ministers, each of whom represented 1 town in the colony. These 49 men were to judge Anne Hutchinson, who awaited her turn seated on one of the rough, backless benches that held the audience in front of Winthrop.

The governor had ordered the trial to be moved from Boston, where Hutchinson lived with her prosperous husband and 12 children, to the Newtown church and meetinghouse to do more than inconvenience her. Hutchinson had a sizable number of supporters and had effectively split the colony into two factions. Well known as a skilled nurse and midwife and married to a prominent textile merchant, Hutchinson numbered among her backers former governor Henry Vane, the Reverend John Cotton, the Reverend John Wheelwright, and the majority of Puritans in Boston. However, Winthrop had all the magistrates and ministers from the country and villages surrounding the city on his side, and six months earlier he had defeated Vane in the May 1637 gubernatorial election. Vane sailed home to England in August, dismayed with the political squabbling in the colony. Cotton, troubled by aspects of Hutchinson's thinking, had begun to qualify his support. Winthrop seized his advantage, called Wheelwright and Hutchinson to trial, and moved the proceedings to an outlying district.

He put the second part of his strategy into action on November 2, during the selection of deputies. The General Court's first business had been to examine each deputy's credentials. One by one, Winthrop and his supporters quickly dismissed any member found to be a Hutchinson adherent. The remaining group of deputies were among the wealthiest and most powerful men in the entire colony—and only two were disposed in Hutchinson's favor.

Approximately one week after the deputies were selected, the court began to hear cases of individuals connected to Hutchinson. The audience listened as Winthrop accused the Reverend Wheelwright of being the cause of "present troubles and disturbances," disenfranchised him (deprived him of citizenship—the right to vote or hold office), and commanded him to leave the colony within two weeks. John Coggeshall, a Hutchinson supporter, was disenfranchised. The banishment of another of Hutchinson's close associates, William Aspinwall, followed. The mood of the court was clear when Winthrop rose from his seat and proclaimed, "The Court calls Mistress Anne Hutchinson." (Dialogue from the trial is taken from court records, from Winthrop's own journal, and from a transcription made by an anonymous friend of Anne's.)

Hutchinson, clad in a long dark dress with white collar and cuffs, her graying hair modestly covered with a white cap, rose and faced the thin, patrician governor. She knew the trial would be an ordeal. In a community dedicated to live according to God's law as revealed in the Bible and led by ministers, legal proceedings and arguments were sure to be intricate, sometimes confusing, and based on sophisticated interpretations of Scripture. Decades ago in En-gland, Hutchinson's father, Francis Marbury, had been forced to argue his case before officials similarly well versed in religion. He had given his daughter an unusually thorough education, including accounts of his defense. Ably equipped for her own trial, Hutchinson clutched a worn leather-bound Bible that she had studied for years and prepared to defend herself as Winthrop began:

Mrs. Hutchinson, you are called here as one of those that have troubled the peace of the commonwealth and the churches. You are known to be a woman that hath had a great share in the promoting of those opinions that are causes of this trouble, and to be joined in affinity and affection with some of those the court hath taken notice of and passed censure upon. You have spoken divers[e] things, as we have been informed, very prejudicial to the honor of the churches and ministers. You have maintained a meeting in your house that hath been condemned by the General Assembly as a thing not tolerable, nor comely in the sight of God, nor fitting for your sex, and notwithstanding that was cried down you have continued the same.

Therefore we have thought good to send for you to understand how things are, that if you be in an erroneous way we may reduce [punish] you that so you may become a profitable member here among us. Otherwise if you be obstinate then the court may take such course that you may trouble us no further.

Ignoring his threat to reduce her to become a profitable member, Hutchinson replied calmly, "I am called here

When the first colonists arrived in the Massachusetts Bay Colony in 1630, the area was a wilderness. They quickly constructed simple, primitive buildings of wood and mud, such as the First Church of Boston, shown as it appeared from 1630 to 1640.

to answer before you but I hear no things laid to my charge."

Surprised by the direct challenge, Winthrop asserted that he had already stated some charges and could tell her more.

"Name one, sir," Hutchinson shot back.

In response, the governor repeated his claim that Hutchinson had approved of and encouraged the dissidents who had already come before the court, been tried, and sentenced.

Intelligent and unafraid of speaking her mind, Hutchinson responded, "That's a matter of conscience, sir. . . . What law have I broken?"

Winthrop accused her of breaking the Fifth Commandment, "Honor thy

father and mother," which the Puritans interpreted as a command to obey the rulers of the colony. Hutchinson argued that she did in fact honor them.

This angered Winthrop. He snapped, "We do not mean to discourse with those of your sex . . . you do endeavor to set forward this faction and so you do dishonor us."

Then Winthrop turned to the subject of the afternoon religious meetings Hutchinson held and proclaimed that she had no right to preach, even within her own home. Two months before in an attempt to silence her, a law had been passed stating that all large meetings of women were disorderly and should cease.

Hutchinson had continued holding the assemblies. Her primary purpose had been to discuss the weekly sermons of John Cotton, a minister and teacher at First Church of Boston. But before long she had begun to speak about her own understanding of Puritanism and to criticize ministers who held differing interpretations. Those who listened to her and agreed with her began to stand up and walk out of church when a sermon displeased them. Some services turned into shouting matches. Her departure from doctrine and the ensuing threat to established preachers had made several ministers angry enough to join with Winthrop in bringing Hutchinson to trial.

Hutchinson did not address these underlying issues. She replied that there was no law against private assembly and explained that she began holding women's meetings only after a friend warned that church officials frowned upon her absence from similar meetings held by other women. She quoted a biblical verse from the Book of Titus that read in part, "the elder women shall instruct the younger," to justify her actions.

Winthrop, not satisfied with her answer, asked about the men who came to her house. Hutchinson denied that men attended her meetings. Trying a different tack, Winthrop countered: "Suppose a man should come and say, 'Mrs. Hutchinson, I hear that you are a woman that God hath given his grace unto and you have knowledge in the word of God. I pray, instruct me a little.' Ought you not to instruct this man?"

Hutchinson baited him. "I think I may. . . . You tell me I may not teach women, and yet you ask me to instruct the court?"

Winthrop bellowed in rage, "We do not call you to teach the court but to lay open yourself."

A wave of exhaustion washed over Hutchinson, and she looked as if she were about to faint. Her travels had been difficult and she had been standing in the cold for hours facing her inquisitors. The ordeal was excruciating for a 46-year-old woman in her fifth month of pregnancy. Hutchinson had not complained once, but the court allowed her to sit for the remainder of the trial.

Hutchinson refused to address the issue of teaching men or admit that she had done anything wrong. Instead, she quoted another scriptural passage about a woman and her husband teaching a man who came to them for instruction. She also asked if any rule existed that told her to turn women away that came to her seeking help.

Winthrop countered with a shout, "What rule have you to teach them!" Claiming she had cited two verses in the Bible that ruled she could indeed teach others, she noted wryly, "Must I shew [show] my name written therein?"

Winthrop next attacked Hutchinson for inciting religious disharmony and stirring up political dissent. He exploded, "Your course is not to be suffered for we feel it to be greatly prejudicial to the State! We see not that any should set up any other exercises besides what authority hath already set up. . . . Your opinions are known to be different from the word of God and you have seduced many simple souls. Those that have frequented your meetings are flown off from ministers and magistrates. . . . We see no rule of God for this! We must therefore put this course away from you or restrain you from maintaining it."

Hutchinson denied the accusation that the theological concepts she espoused differed from the accepted beliefs of Puritanism, although in fact they did. She stated that Winthrop and her accusers could silence her only if they could find a rule from Scriptures allowing them to do so.

Winthrop thundered back, "We are your judges, and not you ours and we must compel you to it."

John Winthrop was a well-respected lawyer in England when he joined 11 other men to charter the Massachusetts Bay Company to colonize New England. An intelligent, complex man and a prolific writer, he served several terms as governor and kept a detailed journal that provides invaluable facts about and insights into the early decades of the colony.

As yet, Winthrop had made little headway with his arguments and not one of the other 49 members of the court had spoken a word. Winthrop allowed his deputy governor, Thomas Dudley, to continue the trial.

First, Dudley restated the charges against Hutchinson. Then, he introduced a new accusation: Hutchinson, he said, had insulted all the colony's ministers by claiming they preached a "covenant of works" and were thus not among the Lord's elect. According to Hutchinson, Dudley said, only the Reverend Cotton walked in a "covenant of grace"; only he was among the Lord's elect.

The difference between a covenant of grace and a covenant of works was at the center of the theological controversy surrounding Hutchinson. The concepts were the subject of learned discourse and intricate arguments. Puritans believed every person was sinful and would be doomed to hell, except for the intervention of God, who had bestowed grace on certain individuals (the elect) through the Holy Spirit. Those individuals were saved, and their pious life and adherence to biblical commands marked them as sanctified. Hutchinson felt that most of the clergy were overly concerned with exhorting their listeners to perform works of charity, live piously, work hard, and strictly obey scriptural law, which would show that they had been saved. She believed that salvation (the state of grace) was more than a matter of works; rather it was a gift from the Holy Spirit, which dwelled in each individual saved soul. Good deeds were meaningless unless the person received the free grace of God and felt the spirit dwelling within.

At her meetings she had begun to disparage ministers who stressed following scriptural law over the importance of the presence of the Holy Spirit. Before long, as Winthrop noted in his journal, "it began to be as common . . . to distinguish between men by being under a covenant of grace or a covenant of works, as in other countries between Protestants and Papists [Catholics]." Hutchinson claimed outright that most of the Puritan ministers, except for the Reverends Cotton and Wheelwright, were unfit to preach.

When faced with Dudley's accusation, she challenged him to prove his charge. He asserted that Hutchinson held the opinion that "if they [the Puritan clergy] do not preach a covenant of grace clearly, then they preach a covenant of works."

Hutchinson responded firmly, "No Sir, one may preach a covenant of grace more clearly than another, so I said."

Deputy Governor Dudley and the ministers were not appeased by her clever answer. They were determined to break Hutchinson and redeem the ministry she had criticized so clearly. Persecuted in England for their religious views and forced to leave by King Charles, Puritan ministers in New En-

gland treasured the power they had in their respective parishes. The thought that a woman could draw their parishioners away was intolerable.

Dudley tried again. "I do but ask you this, when the ministers do preach a covenant of works do they preach a way of salvation?"

Feeling this was a vague question, Hutchinson refused to answer. Winthrop interrupted to comment acidly that Hutchinson obviously knew when to speak and when to hold her tongue.

The day had grown dark; the trial had taken hours. Gaunt, leafless trees cast long shadows over the paths of frozen mud outside the meetinghouse, and the wind grew more bitterly cold. Candles, made by hand, were too valuable to waste, and oil lamps were scarce, so the prosecution ended for the day. A frustrated Winthrop announced to Hutchinson that the court had offered her the opportunity to admit her wrongs, but she had refused and it had grown too late to continue. He told her the court wished to give her "a little more time to consider of it" and expected to see her the next morning.

Hutchinson had but one night to "consider of" all that she had said and done since her arrival in New England three years ago and all that had transpired in the trial thus far. She had one more night to prepare the remainder of her defense and, perhaps, to sleep.

ANNO · ETATIS   SVÆ · XLIX ·

*King Henry VIII, who ruled England from 1509 to 1547, separated
from the Roman Catholic church and made himself head of the
Church of England in 1534 in order to divorce his wife Catherine of
Aragon, who had borne him no male heir, and legally marry his
pregnant mistress, Anne Boleyn. His act unleashed a century and a
half of religious and political turmoil in England.*

T W O

Minister's Daughter

Anne, the third child born to Bridget Dryden Marbury and Francis Marbury, was christened on July 20, 1591, in the tiny market town of Alford, Lincolnshire, about 125 miles north of London, England. It was usual at the time to wait until children were three days old to baptize them, for infant mortality was high. Bridget had borne Francis Marbury two children before Anne, only one of whom, John, survived. By his first wife, Elizabeth Moore, who died around 1587, Francis Marbury had three daughters, two of whom, Susan and Elizabeth, were still living when Anne was born.

Francis Marbury supported his household by teaching school and preaching at St. Wilfred's Church, where most of the religious, political, and social business of the region was transacted. Home to a few hundred people, Alford was ringed by even smaller parishes, farms, and manors, including Bilsby, Mawthorpe, Rigsby,

and Saleby. Farmers and housewives could easily walk from these outlying areas to Alford's church and market. Beyond these quiet communities, the broad, flat plains of East Anglia stretched to the North Sea. Peaceful Alford appeared untouched by the recent tumult of English history. Yet Anne's father and her mother's relatives had been deeply affected by the religious convulsions of 16th-century England, which had begun nearly half a century before Anne's birth.

In 1529, King Henry VIII of England sought to have his marriage to Catherine of Aragon ruled invalid by the Catholic church, for she had had no son, and Henry wanted a male heir. Enraged by the pope's refusal to annul his marital bond, Henry established the Church of England, with himself as its head, by the Act of Supremacy in 1534. He promptly approved his own divorce, seized monasteries and church lands, ruthlessly suppressed any opposition to his position as supreme head of the church, and married a total of six wives in his fruitless quest for a son. A decade of unrest followed his death, until Henry and Anne Boleyn's daughter took the throne as Elizabeth I in 1558.

One of the most influential monarchs in European history, Elizabeth presided over years of peace and prosperity, the growth of England as a naval power, a remarkable age of literature, and the beginning of explorations in the New World. She dealt firmly with religious disputes that threatened to mar her reign. Her own Act of Supremacy made her the head of the Church of England in 1559, and she soon promulgated the Thirty-nine Articles of the Anglican Faith, determined to establish uniform, official doctrines and beliefs in response to the growth of reform movements.

Many English ministers had been inspired by the European Protestant movements that swept Europe after Martin Luther, a German priest and theologian, broke with Catholicism in 1517, protesting corruption in the Roman Catholic church. When their own monarch confirmed their independence from Rome, some clergymen enthusi-

Queen Elizabeth I, the only child of Henry VIII and Anne Boleyn, is carried by court dignitaries on a journey to Blackfriars. Anne Marbury was born during the reign of Elizabeth I, who ruled for 45 years and presided over the growth of England as both a world power and a Protestant nation.

astically embraced the opportunity to profoundly reform church and society. They sought to move Anglicanism even further from the influence of Roman Catholicism—to purify it of any taint. But Queen Elizabeth maintained control over her church, not hesitating to persecute, imprison, and execute Puritans (as the reformers were called) who she thought went too far. In addition, she not only quelled the Catholic rebellions and plots that troubled her nation throughout her reign but also supported Protestants against Catholics in other European countries. By 1588, her policies led Philip II, the staunchly Catholic king of Spain, to attempt an invasion to quash English Protestantism. His fleet of ships, the Spanish Armada, was soundly defeated, establishing England's accession to the first rank of European powers.

Anne Marbury was born amid the optimism following this triumph. Her mother, Bridget Dryden, was a daughter of John Dryden, owner of Canons Ashby, a substantial estate in Northamptonshire. The Dryden family tree included wealthy property owners, members of the landed gentry, and several nobles. Many were active in politics, and a considerable number were Puritans. One of Bridget's relatives had been imprisoned in the Tower of London several times for his attempts at religious reform.

Francis Marbury was born in 1556. His family were prominent landowners, and he attended Cambridge University for a time, although he left in 1571 before earning a degree. He then be-

came an Anglican minister in Northampton but displeased the church hierarchy before long. A learned, highly intelligent man, he had no patience with clerics he considered badly trained or unqualified. His frank and public criticism soon earned him a prison sentence, but after his release he returned to the fight. Demanding that better education and training be required for the clergy and that the Church of England provide more ordained ministers so every parish church could have its own rector, he insulted bishops by claiming they were stupid themselves for appointing ignorant ministers. In 1578, he was brought to trial before the High Commission in London, an assembly of religious authorities appointed by Queen Elizabeth to maintain uniformity in the Church of England. In spite of his able, spirited defense, he was again thrown in jail. Upon his release from Marshalsea Prison he accepted a living (a steady job that provided room and board) at St. Wilfred's and married Bridget Dryden.

In 1590, just before Anne was born, Francis's honesty and disputatious nature led to a renewal of his old difficulties. He had begun to denounce clerics who abused their position for personal gain, and powerful bishops deemed his criticisms to be a challenge to the Church of England and Queen Elizabeth herself. The hierarchy responded by depriving him of his post at St. Wilfred's and accusing him of insolence and Puritanism. Age and responsibilities to his growing family may have led to his decision to claim he was not a

A view of a small village in Essex, one of many that dotted the fields of England. Anne was born in such a community, the tiny market town of Alford, to Bridget and Francis Marbury in July 1591.

Puritan and instead a good member of the Church of England. His denial saved him from prison, but he was forced to endure several years of enforced silence before he could preach again.

Francis passed the time by attending to his property and farms and tutoring Anne, who quickly learned to read. Acquiring this skill was an immeasurable advantage to the young girl, for many women in 16th-century England were illiterate. Anne was fortunate to grow up under the rule of Queen Elizabeth, who had enjoyed an excellent education herself and strongly believed in instructing women. Under her encouraging policies, the rate of female literacy was higher than ever before in England or ever again until the late 19th century.

Anne's early reading assignments included the Bible and her father's account of his 1578 trial, which he had had printed and published. Among other ecclesiastical works in Francis Marbury's library were papers asserting that properly educated women would be capable of entering the ministry—an extremely radical concept that may

James VI of Scotland ascended to the throne of England as James I in 1603. His battles with Puritan reformers and Parliament made his reign a stormy one.

have affected Anne. Her proud, independent father imparted more than knowledge; from her later actions it appears that he bequeathed her the courage to challenge authority as well.

All the while, Anne's mother, Bridget Marbury, continued to perform the myriad household duties of an Elizabethan wife while almost continually in some stage of pregnancy. After having Anne, Bridget bore 12 more children, and as soon as Anne was old enough to help supervise the growing brood, she did. Children were expected to take on responsibility early, for life in the country required endless work. Bridget Marbury, as other Alford wives did, kept a kitchen garden that provided the household with food and medicines. She taught her daughters the skills they would need throughout their life: how to spin thread, sew and mend the family's clothes, preserve and pickle fruits and vegetables, bake bread, cure meat, and make cheese and butter. In keeping with the charity expected of the wife of a man of property, in addition to maintaining her own household Bridget visited and helped other women in the community—especially when they gave birth, for she was a midwife.

As Anne grew older, she began to accompany her mother on her rounds and learned how to brew herbs, barks, roots, and leaves into the medicinal teas and cordials that were believed to assuage pain and cure various ills. Medical care was not advanced, and doctors were rare and often able to do little to help their patients. A solid knowledge of folk medicine was a great asset, and Anne learned as much about healing from her mother as she learned about reading and writing from her father.

When Queen Elizabeth died on March 24, 1603, Anne was nearly 12. James I, formerly James VI of Scotland, ascended the throne of England. He proclaimed himself king by divine right—a European concept rather unpopular with the English. Eager to establish his own policies and perhaps resentful of his female predecessor's popularity, he showed no inclination to improve the status of women or encourage their education. In 1604 he called on Parliament to enact a stern witchcraft statute that redefined witchcraft as a pact with the devil to inflict harm; the offense was further made punishable by hanging. The king made it clear that witches were almost always female, claiming that of every 21 witches, 20 were women. He and his bishops stated that midwives could not baptize newborns, even in emergencies when no priest was available or when the baby was dying. Women, he held, were weak, evil, and not to be trusted.

That same year he called the Hampton Court Conference to address issues raised by the Puritans. His arrogant, patronizing attitude deeply offended the reformers and soon alienated Parliament as well. As a result of the rigid Anglican orthodoxy James I demanded, many Puritans who held positions in the Church of England were deprived of their post. Puritans in Parliament and others angered by the king's high-handed ways replied by resisting his demands for money to finance his extravagant way of life.

In the summer of 1605, the continuing turmoil directly touched the Marburys of Alford. At the age of 49, Francis Marbury, subdued by a combination of disasters, apparently gave up his efforts to improve the Church of England. That year the plague swept north through Lincolnshire, claiming the lives of three of his young children. Severe inflation gripped the country in the wake of the king's disastrous economic battles with Parliament, and although both Francis and Bridget brought substantial inheritances to their household, buying necessities soon became difficult. The weather collaborated in the dismal state of affairs, and the flat farmland of East Anglia was alternately flooded by storms and afflicted by drought. Francis Marbury needed a living. King James's decision to rid the church of nonconformist ministers left him with a shortage of clergy, particularly in London. Although Marbury had been a troublemaker, he had never openly admitted to being a Puritan. Consequently, he applied for an appointment as a minister and was assigned to the church of St. Martin's in the Vintry, 125 miles away in London.

A dozen Marburys prepared to uproot themselves. No longer would Anne, then 14, her 20-year-old half sister Susan, 15-year-old brother John, and 7 younger siblings enjoy working and playing in the open fields and wandering the country paths of Lincolnshire.

Most of the people they knew had spent their entire life in one small place, seeing only the few hundred inhabitants of Alford. The Marburys were going to join the more than 225,000 people who called crowded London home.

The family had to prepare carefully for the momentous journey. Anne and the older children helped Bridget pack up the furnishings they would take with them. Bundles of clothes, pots, pans, quilts, and comforters were neatly stowed away for the trip. The older Marburys would make the trek on horseback, while Bridget, pregnant once again, and the youngest children traveled in the family carriage, which had to be checked and put in shape for the long ride. Francis acquired the documents permitting him and his household to move from one county to another and to travel the roads, which were often unmarked dirt paths greatly in need of repair. Rain regularly turned the rutted lanes to mud and swelled the streams and rivers that had to be forded (waded through on horseback). The 10-day trip was not only difficult and uncomfortable but also extremely dangerous. Bands of robbers roamed the highways, so the Marburys stayed close to other groups and never traveled after dark. At night, they stayed at inns where as many as five slept in one bed. Each morning they awoke, ate a hearty breakfast (for there were no restaurants along the way), and dressed in layers of clothing to protect themselves from wind and damp.

The clan finally arrived in London

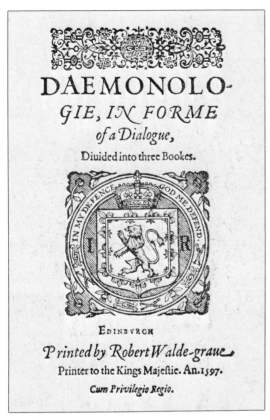

DAEMONOLO-GIE, IN FORME
of a Dialogue,

Diuided into three Bookes.

EDINBVRGH

Printed by Robert Walde-graue,

Printer to the Kings Majeftie. An. 1597.

Cum Privilegio Regio.

Magic and witchcraft fascinated James I. In 1597, he published his Daemonologie, *a treatise on "Magic in general, and Necromancie in special . . . of Sorcerie and Witchcraft" and "all these kindes of spirits, and spectres that appeares and troubles persones." Annoyed by comparison to and praise of his female predecessor, Elizabeth I, James revealed his misogynist sentiments in his assertion that the ranks of witches contained 20 times more women than men.*

safe from robbers and mishaps on the road and moved into the rectory of St. Martin's Church. Their new home was typical of most rectories at the time and featured comfortable rooms, adequate space, and sturdy furniture. Although the house was not dissimilar from the one they left in Alford, the surrounding city presented a great contrast to the quiet market town where Anne had grown up. London was the largest industrial center in England, a major port, and the center of government and religion. A vast range of goods from abroad and all over the country were for sale; an enormous variety of people bustled about the streets. Anyone with wealth, social influence, or political ambitions either lived in London or maintained a second residence there. News, ideas, and fashion—all emanated from the busy capital.

For Anne, life would never be the same. She became accustomed to new accents, milder weather, and large crowds. London was cramped, and its clogged streets were full of tradesmen's carts, nobles' coaches, and street criers of all types. Along the sides were small shops on top of which sat narrow houses, sometimes four or five stories high. The upper floors often jutted out over the roads and alleys, cutting off the sunlight. Anne had enjoyed broad vistas, fresh air, and open space in Alford; London could not offer these amenities. But London gave Anne much that Alford could not. Ships from many lands unloaded exotic flowers, fruits, plants, and fine fabrics. Anne and her mother could purchase then-exotic foods such as peaches, olives, and almonds to add to the family larder. But far more important to Anne, ships

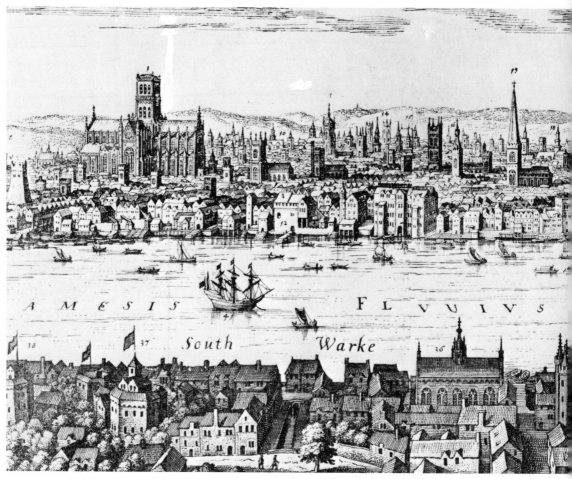

A 1630 view of London shows its waterfront crammed with buildings. In 1605, Anne, her parents, and her nine brothers and sisters moved to London. An important port and the center of England's social, political, and cultural life, the crowded city offered a wealth of new experiences to the Marbury clan.

also brought people with new ideas, and to her delight she found she could buy books on almost every subject at the numerous bookstalls or from itinerant peddlers.

Religious tumult continued and dramatically came to the forefront of national attention within weeks of Marbury's installation in October as minister at St. Martin's. On November 5, 1605, five fanatic Catholics, angered by King James's failure to order greater toleration of their religion, planned to blow up Parliament and the king. Guy Fawkes, one of the conspirators, was caught in the cellar below Parliament's

During the next five years, Francis Marbury benefited from this state of affairs and received increasingly important appointments in London in addition to the ministry at St. Martin's.

For Anne, living in London as a prominent minister's daughter broadened her understanding of politics and religion. Each minister of a parish was also the chief of the vestry, a group of influential churchgoers who chose parishioners not only to fill positions of power in church affairs but also in the secular community. From observing this process, Anne learned about local politics.

Eventually, Anne's older half sister married and left home. As the eldest unmarried daughter, Anne was then permitted to sit at the table when guests were invited to dinner. Although she was not allowed to speak, she listened carefully to the conversations and learned quite a bit about the larger questions of English religion and politics from her silent vantage point. Puritans and their agitations had become a topic of conversation nearly everywhere, and Marbury's dinner table was no exception. In addition to attempting to purify the Anglican church and its religious rites from any lingering Catholic influence, Puritans had begun to question the infallibility of the king. Parliament was dominated by Puritans, who resented James's unceasing demands for money and his numerous speeches on the divine right of monarchs. Anne listened to her mother's Puritan relatives talk about the trouble they planned to give King James.

chambers, guarding the 36 barrels of gunpowder the group had hidden there 6 months earlier. He and the others involved were arrested, tried, tortured, and executed with great cruelty in the winter of 1606. After the attempt, known as the Gunpowder Plot, England rejoiced at the king's deliverance, and even the increasingly Puritan Parliament voted an ample subsidy to finance James's lavish expenditures. On the king's part, he grew more favorable to all his loyal, non-Catholic subjects.

While she lived in London, Anne came into contact with two groups of religious reformers more radical than Puritans: Familists and Separatists. Women had played key roles in the beginning of the Puritan movement and were more important still in Familism and Separatism. Familism was a controversial sect condemned by orthodox clergy. It had been founded among Protestants in Holland and was quickly exported across the North Sea to East Anglia and London. Its members embraced the idea that every individual believer (both female and male) could enjoy direct communication with God and benefited from the presence of the Holy Spirit as a guiding light within the soul. Each person in the Family of Love (as its members preferred to be called) was wholly responsible for his or her own actions, for they rejected the doctrine of predestination (the belief that God had ordained at the beginning of time which individuals would be saved and which would be damned). Even more shocking to Christians of that era, Familists did not believe in the concept of original sin (the idea that all infants were born as sinners and could be saved only through the grace of God). Anne learned more about Familism later but first became acquainted with the sect in London.

The Separatists were not as extreme in their beliefs as Familists. They were Puritans who felt attempts to purify and reform the Church of England were futile. They believed that a complete separation from the Anglican church was necessary and sought to emigrate in order to found a church of their own and to escape harassment and persecution. Approximately a hundred of them planned to set sail from Boston, the major port of Lincolnshire, in 1607, but authorities prevented them from doing so. They waited until 1608, when they were allowed to leave for Holland. The Marburys' connections to Lincolnshire remained strong, and they heard much of the travails of the Separatists, or Pilgrims, as their leader William Bradford sometimes called them.

Anne knew of the growth of numerous sects and listened to disputes over doctrines and politics, but she could not take part. In contrast, as her brothers grew older they prepared to take their place in the world. Although they were tutored at home as she had been, three of them eventually completed their education at Oxford University. Anne remained at home, continuing to learn from her father and helping her mother supervise servants and maintain the ever-larger number of Marburys. She even assisted her mother during the births of three more siblings: Thomas, who died young, was born in 1606 and followed by Anthony in 1608 and Katherine in 1610. Anne grew quite close to her youngest sister and carefully watched over her education.

Early in 1611, Francis Marbury died at the age of 55. Not quite 20 years old, Anne mourned the loss of her beloved father, who had encouraged her intellect and independence. She had little time to grieve openly; she had to help care for her 10 younger brothers and

Separatists depart from the docks. Dubbed "Pilgrims" by William Bradford, their leader, they chose to leave both the Anglican church and England, finally making their way to Holland in 1609. At her father's well-attended dinners, Anne heard stories of the Pilgrims' mistreatment at the hands of the religious and governmental authorities.

sisters, whose ages ranged from 1 to 17. The number was sadly reduced when 9-year-old Daniel died on September 19, 1611.

In his will, dated January 30, 1611, Francis Marbury left each of his 12 children 200 British marks (a substantial amount), which they would receive upon reaching the adult age of 21. At that time, his sons could choose to stay with their mother or establish themselves elsewhere. However, all young females were to remain at home until they came under the guardianship of a husband. For the next year and a half, because a new minister took over the pulpit and the rectory of St. Martin's in the Vintry, Anne lived with her mother and the rest of her brothers and sisters in another parish in London, called Saint Mary Woolchurch Haw and Saint Mary Woolnoth. By the standards of 16th-century England, Anne was rather old to remain unmarried. Yet her ability to run a large household, skill in medicine, and considerable inheritance were valuable assets and ensured that she would not remain single for long.

Anne married William Hutchinson in August 1612 and returned to live in Alford. The imposing spire of St. Botolph's Church rose above the Lincolnshire plains in Boston 24 miles away, and the Hutchinsons made the long journey there as often as they could to hear the Reverend John Cotton preach.

THREE

Alford Housewife

On August 9, 1612, Anne Marbury married 26-year-old William Hutchinson, a wealthy sheep farmer and textile merchant whom she had known since her childhood in Alford. Although no recorded evidence proves that the two had remained in touch after Anne moved away from Alford, William very probably saw her when he made business visits to London, the center of English commerce. The Hutchinsons were well-established tradespeople, and William's grandfather John had been mayor of Lincoln. One of John's five sons, Edward, moved to Alford and established a thriving fabric business a short time after Francis Marbury arrived at St. Wilfred's. William, the oldest of Edward's 10 children, was born in 1586 and followed the trade of his father.

Anne and William suited each other very well. Unlike the majority of married couples of the time, they maintained a mutual respect for one another and, most surprisingly, treated each other as equals. Over the years their devotion never wavered.

Shortly after the wedding, recorded in the parish church of Saint Mary Woolchurch Haw and Saint Mary Woolnoth, the Hutchinsons departed for Alford, where they began setting up their new household. William was a wealthy man, and Anne brought a good-sized inheritance to the union. They were able to move into a substantial house, much like the home of William's parents. Their new house featured several bedrooms, a dining room, a study, a parlor, and rooms for the many tasks required to maintain a household. These included a large kitchen, a pantry, a buttery where cheese and butter were prepared, and several outbuildings for milking cows, brewing ale, and storing wool. A stable completed the establishment. William Hutchinson outfitted his home with furnishings that attested to his afflu-

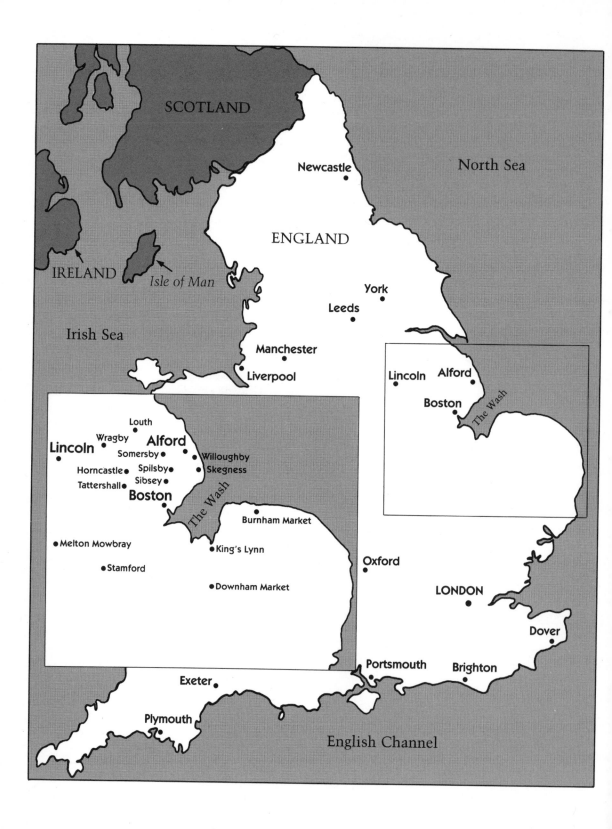

ence: canopy-covered beds, plenty of cupboards, chairs, tables, books, candlesticks, and linens for every purpose. Anne was proud to possess a kitchen fully equipped with a variety of iron, pewter, and copper pots and pans. The newlyweds even had a wooden bathtub.

Less than a year after their marriage, they watched as their first child, Edward, was baptized on May 28, 1613. Anne and William expected to have a large family; William had 5 brothers and 4 sisters, and Anne's mother had borne 15 children. Because nearly half of all infants died before the age of three, women bore children one after another, unsure how many might survive to adulthood. Anne gave birth to Susanna in 1614, Richard in 1615, Faith in 1617, Bridget in 1619, Francis in 1620, Elizabeth in 1622, William in 1623 (who died young), Samuel in 1624, Anne in 1626, Mary in 1628, and Katherine in 1630. Three more—a second William, another Susanna, and Zuriel—followed in the 1630s.

The Hutchinsons lived in Alford for 22 years. Neither kept a diary, but their parish register records the birth date of each of their children, and historical records provide information about life in Lincolnshire during this period. The

Alford is located near the east coast of England, where the North Sea cuts into the land and forms an area known as the Wash. Boston, to the south, was Lincolnshire's major port until its harbor on the Wash became so filled with silt that large boats were no longer able to use it.

years appear to have been busy ones for the Hutchinsons. William labored to provide for his growing brood, and his textile enterprise thrived. Anne supervised the housekeeping and bore a child about every 18 months. Like her mother before her, Anne not only provided experienced medical care for her family but also assisted neighborhood women as a midwife and healer. She was competent and energetic—that all but one of her children survived their childhood is a testament to her skill. Also, despite the numerous duties that filled Anne's days, as the educated daughter of an established minister she found time to keep up with the latest tempestuous developments in the Church of England.

Sects proliferated amid the political turmoil at the beginning of the 17th century. King James I, enraged by Parliament's refusal to approve more funds for his extravagant way of life, dissolved the legislative body in 1611, and it met again only once in the next decade. Consequently, when disputes about Puritanism and royal finances arose, they were not settled. Radicals and nonconformists, as those who did not comply with Anglican doctrine were known, became more numerous, and one area in Cambridgeshire, the Isle of Ely, became especially well known as a home for dissenters. Among them were several women preachers, one of whom, known only as the Woman of Ely, greatly impressed Anne, who later praised her as a "woman of a thousand, hardly any like her." Although Anne was certainly aware of this radical preacher and other divisive sects, she never traveled the 60 miles between Alford and Ely to hear the woman speak. Apparently, she could find controversy closer to home. A contemporary historian, Thomas Edwards, recorded the existence of the Woman of Ely and added: "There are also some woman preachers in our times, who keep constant lectures, preaching weekly to many men and women. In Lincolnshire, in Holland and those parts there is a woman preacher who preaches (it's certain), and 'tis reported also she baptizeth, but that's not so certain."

Some of these women may have been Familists, members of the group Anne had encountered in London. Familism was spreading, especially among businessmen, but the Hutchinsons were not among the group's adherents. While Familism, Separatism, and other sects flourished in the disorder that grew under King James's rule, the Hutchinsons remained members of the Church of England. They were greatly attracted to the preaching of one minister in particular: the new vicar at St. Botolph's Church in Boston, only 24 miles to the south.

The Reverend John Cotton had arrived at St. Botolph's on July 12, 1612, a month before the Hutchinsons were married. The 28-year-old minister had a reputation for eloquence, a brilliant background, and a definite inclination toward Puritanism. Cotton's impressive academic career began with his admission to Trinity College at Cambridge University at the age of 13. Upon graduating and receiving his baccalaureate, he had been accepted as a fellow at Emmanuel College in the same university, from which he received his master of arts degree in 1606. For the next few years, he moved steadily upward from tutor to head lecturer to dean. He was ordained an Anglican priest in 1610, and two years later, he became minister of St. Botolph's Church at Boston, a beautiful, imposing structure nearly the size of a cathedral, with a soaring spire that could be seen for miles. It was a prestigious but daunting appointment. According to contemporary accounts, Boston, a town "so famous for religion," boasted a church not only famed for its loveliness but also for its congregation—known far and wide as "factious people," prone to arguments and dissent.

Anne Hutchinson probably first heard stories of Cotton and the Boston parishioners while shopping at the weekly market held in Alford. Each Tuesday, the inhabitants were joined by country dwellers and merchants from various towns who gathered at the colorful collection of stalls set up in the center of town. They brought their produce to sell, looked for bargains from butchers and fishmongers, haggled over the price of clothing and various wares, and greatly enjoyed exchanging information and gossip about their neighbors. Traveling middlemen and retailers brought tales from distant London and beyond. It was here that Hutchinson learned about the latest news, trends, and rumors. Twice a year, in the late spring and late fall, Alford

John Calvin (center, standing) argues a point of doctrine at the Council of Geneva in 1549. Along with Martin Luther, Calvin was one of the great figures of the Protestant Reformation. Puritans based their theology on his teachings, especially his monumental book Institutes of the Christian Religion.

hosted a large, week-long fair where a more extensive array of goods were offered, including the latest printed pamphlets and books about controversies of the day.

Since the founding of the Anglican church, various reform movements had arisen and diminished. The Puritans began by attempting to cleanse the Church of England of Catholic forms of ceremony and worship and to eliminate the hierarchy inherited from the Catholic church, in which dioceses overseen by bishops were divided into parishes run by priests. In time, Puritans sought to reform the Anglican system of belief

as well, bringing it closer to Protestant religious thought in Europe, particularly as taught by John Calvin, an important French theologian who established a religious community in Geneva, Switzerland. Cotton devoted much of his thought to this theological effort. He once said of Protestant writers, "I have read the fathers, and the schoolmen and Calvin too, but I find that he that has Calvin has them all."

The dogma that Calvin espoused in *Institutes of the Christian Religion*, the book that systemized Protestant belief, emphasized predestination, the idea of divine grace, and the concept of the covenant (God's pact with human-kind). Calvin, like other Christian thinkers, held that all humans were born in sin, a result of Adam and Eve's original sin, for which they were expelled from paradise. Calvin differed from Catholic teaching (which did not endorse predestination) in his conclusion that God had elected some souls to be saved and condemned some to be damned—the doctrine of double predestination. He also asserted that because humans were innately sinful, no actions of their own could lead to salvation; only through divine grace could an individual be saved. Puritans struggled with two complicated theological problems that arose from their understanding of Calvin: If an all-knowing God had predestined the saved and the damned, was there any way that humans, with their imperfect understanding, could be assured of their own salvation? If God had complete authority over who was saved and who was damned, how could humankind have any moral responsibility—what was the use of trying to behave rightly?

Cotton and the Puritans labored over this dilemma. According to the covenant theology adopted by Puritans, God's original contract with humans was called the covenant of works—by obeying God's laws, humans obtained salvation and eternal life. When Adam broke this contract, he and all humanity after him were unable to perform any works pleasing to God. Then, taking pity on sinful humans, God offered the covenant of grace—by placing their faith in Jesus Christ, the saved (or elect)

could consent to accept divine grace, which would enable them to perform good works. With the gift of grace came the capacity for moral action, for constantly trying to live in the right manner (which the Puritans understood as studying the Bible and obeying its laws) was the mark of the elect. The saved were charged with attempting to live correctly, and the ability to do so assured them of their sanctification. Cotton deemed it important, however, not to rely too heavily on works as proof of salvation, for he thought that some could appear to follow the path of salvation without feeling the true spirit in their soul. He stated that true believers knew they were sanctified by an awareness of the spirit within them. Unlike Puritan preachers who thundered tales of humanity's total unworthiness and warnings of damnation from the pulpit, he tended to stress God's love and mercy in offering the covenant of grace to sinful humankind and to deemphasize the role of good works as a preeminent mark of the saved. Anne found both these inclinations in Cotton's ministry very appealing.

A lively market on the outskirts of London is filled with merrymakers. Scores of farmers and housewives from surrounding areas, eager for news as well as bargains, flocked to the Tuesday market at Alford. Traders and merchants who traveled from town to town—from Alford on Tuesday to Boston on Thursday, then south to Essex and London—spread word of the latest doings throughout the kingdom.

Cotton drew support from many quarters. The fourth earl of Lincoln, Theophilus Fiennes-Clinton, was a devout Puritan and Cotton's patron. The dissenters and nonconformists who filled Boston found their minister's ideas attractive as well, although Cotton's Anglican superiors occasionally thought he leaned too far toward Puritanism. Most Bostonians boldly disregarded calls for orthodoxy, however, for they were not kindly disposed toward authority. Their port was gradually becoming unusable, for silt was accumulating and making the water too shallow for large trading ships. When they appealed to King James for help, he ignored them. Angered by the king's lack of response, the townspeople were prone to disregard official pronouncements, whether royal or religious.

Boston found its minister's nonconformist leanings pleasing; Anne admired both the substance and style of his preaching. Although Cotton loved to spend hours in his study poring over learned theological tracts, he was no hermit isolated behind a wall of obscure books. In St. Botolph's pulpit he showed himself to be a gifted orator who crafted well-written sermons and delivered them masterfully. His elocution could move his listeners to tears or uplift them with the promise of God's mercy and grace.

Anne and her husband traveled to hear Cotton as frequently as possible, for there was no pastor in Alford, and St. Wilfred's relied on resident lecturers. Anne held assemblies in her own home to discuss sermons and the Bible and in time attracted quite a following, but this could not compare to hearing Cotton preach the doctrines she found so congenial. Hutchinson could listen to Cotton often while she stayed in Boston, for his popularity led him to begin giving more sermons. He took to the pulpit six times a week: To the regular five-hour Sunday service he added an afternoon session, along with early morning orations on Wednesdays and Fridays, lectures on Saturday afternoons, and discourses on Thursdays, when Boston's market was held. William worked hard at expanding his business, despite the economic troubles that had begun to affect Alford. He could profitably use the time in Boston to attend sheep markets and fairs and to negotiate with fabric merchants there.

Despite the advantages, both spiritual and worldly, of a visit to Boston, the Hutchinsons had to plan each visit carefully. Traveling the 48-mile round-trip took 3 days—a day and a half each way. They usually planned to spend three or four days there, and Anne had to find a caretaker to watch over her young children, while William had to find someone he trusted to run the day-to-day affairs of his textile enterprise. Despite the travails of the journey, they probably made the trip several times a year.

Popular as Cotton was with his parishioners and churchgoers from outlying areas, such as the Hutchinsons, he ran into trouble with the Anglican hierarchy. Twice his unorthodox actions nearly cost him his living. In 1615, the great number of listeners he attracted drove him to divide the congregation into a large outer circle and a smaller, elite inner circle. Those excluded from the group close to Cotton lost no time in complaining to the diocese, and Cotton was called to account for his actions. With the aid of Thomas Leverett, a member of St. Botolph's who was particularly devoted to Cotton, the affair was smoothed over. Seven years later, in 1622, Cotton was charged and brought to trial in the case of *Thomas Shaw v. Atherton Hough*. The bishops accused Hough and his friends of vandalizing church property and claimed that Cotton's preaching had led them to do so. Once again, Cotton escaped official censure, although the next year he received instructions mandating stricter adherence to biblical texts.

During these years, life grew hectic for the Hutchinsons, especially for Anne. By 1622, she had seven healthy children: four girls and three boys ranging in age from seven to one. In addition to clothing, feeding, and instructing her own offspring, her considerable skills as nurse and midwife ensured that she cared for many others. The training she received from her mother and her own exceptional competence and compassion endeared her to the women of Alford, for few had such experience and skill. She knew much about compounding natural remedies from the herbs and flowers that grew in profusion along the country lanes and

in her own carefully tended garden. Recipes of the time reveal that she probably used parsley to soothe toothaches, mint for colic and other digestive disorders, chamomile for headaches, and many other herbs, each for a different purpose. With each passing year, she became more in demand. Cotton himself noted that she was "well beloved in England at Alford in Lincolnshire (not far from Boston)."

Hutchinson lost her eighth child, William, sometime after his baptism on June 22, 1623. There is no record of his death, but on September 28, 1631, the Hutchinsons gave his name to another son, their 13th child. (Naming a baby after a deceased child was a fairly common custom.) Anne's sorrow did not prevent her from continuing to bear children and help her neighbors, and she perhaps found solace in her own strong faith. She continued to regularly discuss religion and Cotton's sermons with other churchgoers and evidently devoted much thought to Cotton's teachings and her own understanding of theology. By 1625, Cotton's sermons attracted official scrutiny as well.

In the spring of 1625, King James I died. His son Charles acceded to the throne of England as Charles I, accompanied by his Roman Catholic bride, Henrietta Maria of France. William Laud, the archbishop of London, was a favorite of the king's and a firm foe of Puritanism. He continually harassed the bishop of Lincoln, John Williams, who had formerly overlooked Cotton's

Charles I succeeded his father, James I, on the throne of England in 1625. His battles with Parliament and Puritans led to economic chaos, religious controversy, and the English civil war, which ended with his beheading in 1649. During his reign, emigration to New England burgeoned.

obviously Puritan teaching. Cotton's followers began to fear for their nonconformist minister as Laud's calls for adherence to Anglican doctrine became more frequent and strident.

Economic woes soon afflicted Cotton's parishioners in Boston. By 1626, Charles I was desperate for money, as his father had so often been. Ignoring Parliament and the commonly accepted rights of Englishmen, Charles exacted forced loans from the landed gentry and taxed the merchants. Those who failed to comply with the king's demand for money were imprisoned or stripped of their goods. These actions outraged many, especially businessmen in areas that were suffering an economic downturn, as Lincolnshire was. Records indicate that Atherton Hough and a man named William Coddington, among others in Cotton's congregation, refused to pay the new taxes. Cotton's patron, the earl of Lincoln, spent time incarcerated in the Tower of London for daring to oppose the king's schemes.

Around this time, Anne Hutchinson seriously considered joining the Separatists, the best organized of the radical groups who sought to improve society through religious reform. She had observed them leave for Holland in 1608, seeking to remove themselves entirely from the authority of the Church of England. Twelve years later, disappointed with life in Holland, 102 Separatists set sail in the *Mayflower*, landed on the rocky shore of New England, and founded Plymouth Colony. Anne heard of these adventures with interest, but she and her husband were still closely tied to Cotton, who firmly rejected Separatism in a work published in 1629.

Harder times to come changed many

An imaginative illustration depicts the Separatists pushing offshore in a dinghy to board the Mayflower, *on which they sailed to New England, where they founded Plymouth Colony near Cape Cod in 1620.*

minds. Laud pressed ever more zealously for conformity, and the Hutchinsons' corner of England suffered from a series of storms that flooded the countryside, alternating with episodes of severe drought. Famine and economic upheaval followed. From 1626 to 1632, wool prices declined, which particularly affected southern Lincolnshire; Boston and Alford were among the localities hit hardest. Boston's port declined miserably, and riots broke out when rents, land values, and food prices rose. Charles I revealed himself as an even more inept ruler than his father. By 1630, several of Cotton's wealthier parishioners began to consider abandoning old England—crowded, impoverished, and repressive—for the unpopulated shores of the New World. During that same year, Anne Hutchinson endured tragedy and a trial of faith. Unknown to all, the seeds of controversy were being sown.

John Winthrop (center) arrived in Salem on the Arbella *in 1630.*
Winthrop had been elected governor of the newly founded
Massachusetts Bay Colony by its 11 other founders.

FOUR

From Old England to New

In the fall of 1629, a dozen men, many of them close to the earl of Lincoln, formed the Massachusetts Bay Company. Thomas Dudley, the earl's former steward, Isaac Johnson, the earl's brother-in-law, and John Humphrey, engaged to another sister of the earl, joined with Sir Richard Saltonstall, William Vassall, Nicholas West, Kellam Browne, John Sharpe, Increase Nowell, William Pynchon, William Colburn, and a well-established lawyer named John Winthrop in establishing the company for the purpose of settling in New England. They obtained permission to change their original license for a trading company to a royal charter allowing the settlers to manage the company, organized their expedition, and chose John Winthrop as governor. In March 1630, four ships—the *Arbella*, the *Jewel*, the *Talbot*, and the *Ambrose*—set sail together from Southampton for the New World. Among the voyagers were the Reverend John Wilson, William Aspinwall, and William Coddington, a member of St. Botolph's. The fleet sailed without the Hutchinsons, but the venture would profoundly affect Anne's life.

The Hutchinsons, like many of Cotton's congregation, debated whether to leave or stay in England. Anne and William never made a major decision unless they both agreed. Together, they read many of the pamphlets published to encourage settlement in the New World. The promotional material extolled the pure air, abundance of native fruits and fish, and acres of free land. Anne was interested in accounts that portrayed the new community as one that offered women more opportunities than did England. William was intrigued by the availability of land and the distance between the colony and agents of the Crown. His business, like so many others, suffered tremendously under the taxes imposed by Charles I.

After careful consideration, the

A list of magistrates present at court heads the document that officially named the settlement of Boston. Upon arrival, Winthrop and the company immediately set to work establishing a colonial government.

Hutchinsons decided they must move to New England. However, they could not join the first fleet, for in February 1630, Anne gave birth to their 12th child, Katherine, and neither she nor the baby was ready for the arduous trip thousands of miles across the Atlantic Ocean. In addition, William did not wish to abandon his 66-year-old father, Edward, who had no intention of emigrating.

Cotton traveled to Southampton to preach a sermon to the departing fleet, which bore many of his parishioners. The invitation was an honor, and his speech, "God's Promise to His Plantation," was well received. Cotton had intended to return immediately to St. Botolph's in Boston, but weeks passed without news of his arrival. Nearly a month after he was expected back, Anne was aghast to learn that he and his wife, Elizabeth, had contracted the tertiary ague, a life-threatening condition resembling malaria in which the sufferer endured high fever and uncontrollable shaking every other day. Elizabeth fell into a coma and died; John lay near death.

Very slowly, Cotton recovered from his illness and his grief for his wife, but for the next two years he was unable to resume his duties at St. Botolph's or even return to Boston. He spent an entire year convalescing at the estate of his patron and traveled to London and around England before coming back to Boston in 1632 and marrying a close friend of his dead wife's.

Four months after learning of Cotton's illness, Anne endured tragedy in

The cover of a pamphlet about an outbreak of plague shows a skeleton astride coffins (f's without crossbars should be read as s's). Spread by fleas that fed on infected rats and then on people, the disease was little understood and inspired great fear. An epidemic swept north from London to Alford in 1630; a later outbreak completely devastated London in 1665.

her own home. A plaguelike epidemic swept through Alford beginning in late July, and by the end of October, 102 residents of the small town had succumbed. On September 8, 1630, Susanna, the Hutchinsons's eldest daughter who had just turned 16, was buried in St. Wilfred's churchyard. Anne and William were still in deep mourning when their eight-year-old daughter, Elizabeth, died four weeks later on October 4. Both girls may have been taken by the epidemic.

The death of two of her children and the perilous condition of Cotton made the following winter particularly harsh for Anne. The church offered little solace for her grief, for according to the doctrine of the Church of England, such catastrophes were retribution for sin. During the epidemic of 1630, the bereaved of Alford were required to display on their house a sign with a red cross and the words, "Lord have mercy upon us," alerting passersby to their loss and their sin. Years later Anne spoke of a crisis of faith she endured in England, and it is possible that she referred to this period. She said she was so troubled by the state of the church that she "kept a day of solemn humiliation and pondering." During this period of suffering, Anne particularly missed the kind preaching of Cotton that stressed the freely given grace of God. She had begun to consider most other ministers inferior.

She did meet one minister whose preaching she found congenial. Only one mile from Alford in nearby Bilsby, the Reverend John Wheelwright held forth in the pulpit. His views on the covenant of grace were similar to Cotton's, and he was as outspoken as Cotton and a staunch Puritan. He lost his first wife, and around 1630, he married William Hutchinson's youngest sister, Mary. The presence of an agreeable minister in her own family helped to fill the void Cotton's absence had left in Anne's life.

Wheelwright's arrival was not the only change to affect the Hutchinson household. In both the family circle and the greater world, the upheavals continued. On September 14, 1631, William's father, Edward, died and bequeathed a substantial sum of money to William, his eldest son. Two weeks later, Anne and William's 13th child, William, Jr., was baptized.

The next spring brought a renewal of economic woes. Charles I continued to levy ever higher taxes and renewed his system of exacting forced loans. Anne's uncle was thrown into prison for refusing to pay. William's desire to leave England grew stronger as he realized his inheritance might soon be stripped from him. Anne was anxious to leave also. William Laud was rapidly gaining power in the Church of England. Zealous in his persecution of Puritans, he stepped up his attacks on nonconformists and officially silenced those he did not exile or imprison. Before long, Wheelwright was commanded to cease preaching. Cotton returned at last to St. Botolph's only to be greeted by demands from his superiors that he appear before the Court of High Commission to answer charges of nonconformity. Anne deplored these attacks on her brother-in-law and her favorite minister.

By the spring of 1633, Anne and William laid plans to leave England that summer for the Massachusetts Bay Colony. However, the discovery that

An engraving of a painting by Anthony Van Dyck, court painter to Charles I, portrays William Laud after he became archbishop of Canterbury in 1633. His ruthless persecution of Puritans and Calvinists drove many of them to New England and led to his beheading in 1645 during the English civil war.

Anne was pregnant and expecting in November delayed their departure. They helped their oldest child, 21-year-old Edward, and William Hutchinson's youngest brother, 26-year-old Edward, and his wife, Sarah, prepare for the voyage and precede them to New England.

Cotton was preparing to sail as well, although under more trying circumstances. Pursued by agents of the archbishop commanded to ensure he did not leave England, Cotton put aside his ministerial garments and fled in disguise to London along with two other clergymen in the same predicament. The three renegades successfully eluded Laud's men at the ports and finally made their way onto the *Griffin*, where two of Cotton's parishioners, Thomas Leverett and Atherton Hough, met him. Both men had been closely associated with Cotton and had staunchly supported him during his various troubles. The *Griffin* left port in July 1633.

With Cotton in New England and Wheelwright silenced, Anne faced months without a minister she liked. To make matters worse, William Laud had ascended to the archbishopric of Canterbury, the most powerful position in the Church of England aside from the monarchy. The time had clearly come to abandon old England. Anne persuaded her youngest sister, Katherine, recently wed to Richard Scott, to accompany them to the promised land of New England. William turned the family business over to his younger brother John, who had decided

to take his chances and remain in England.

Anne gave birth in mid-November to a girl she named Susanna, after one of the daughters who died in the epidemic of 1630, and the Hutchinson clan began to pack for New England. Anne and William had made a comfortable home after 20 years of marriage, but the rigors of the journey made it necessary to give away most of what they had. They could carry only a few heirlooms, the necessities of life, and objects such as metal pots and pans that were unobtainable in the colony. Conveying even such a small amount of baggage from Alford to London would be difficult enough.

Finally packed, Anne, William, and their 11 children began the first leg of their journey. Other caravans were on the road, and agents of the Crown did not hesitate to halt them without warning. Charles I was alarmed by the numbers of his subjects who were choosing to abandon their homeland for the colonies. As always, he needed money and had begun to fear that a loss of population meant a loss of revenue. He denied permission to anyone who wanted to leave the country until several ship owners persuaded him that the colonies would produce a profit for the Crown. The Hutchinsons continued on to London to wait for the king to grant them the traveling papers allowing them to leave. The Hutchinsons also had to wait for the announcement of a departure date for the *Griffin*. The ship had made the voyage to New England and back the previous year and required a complete overhauling before it was considered seaworthy again. While they were detained, the Hutchinsons and 10 of their brood found lodging at the home of William Bartholomew and his wife, Mary, who were also Puritans waiting to board the *Griffin*.

So close to leaving at last and surrounded by fellow Puritans, Anne relaxed. She mistakenly assumed that her hosts were as freethinking as Cotton and Wheelwright. Eagerly, she discussed her admiration for Cotton and her own understanding of theology. One day as she and William Bartholomew ambled through the churchyard of St. Paul's Cathedral they discussed the Reverend Thomas Hooker, a Puritan who had preceded them to the New World. Anne mentioned that although she generally did not like his preaching, she had been surprised to hear that in his last sermon before departing he declared that God had revealed to him that England would be destroyed. The revelation did not surprise her, but that Hooker claimed to have experienced any revelation at all was astonishing, for he was stern and more often stressed obedience to scriptural law than the individual's relationship to God and the Holy Spirit. She went on to assert that she herself often received revelations from God directly. Bartholomew said nothing at the time, but he did memorize her every word. Anne made the claim that she "never had any great thing done . . . but it was revealed to her beforehand," which startled Bartholomew. A famous Puritan preacher might affirm that he had been

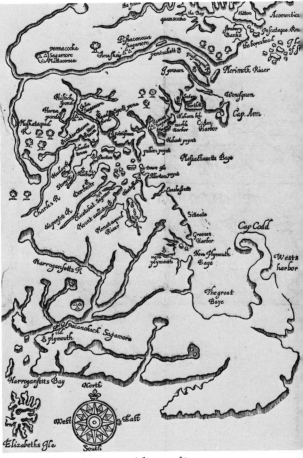

A woodcut of a map (the earliest topographical description of Massachusetts) shows the colony as it appeared the year Anne and William Hutchinson arrived. Boston, Newtown, Roxbury, and Mount Wollaston are clearly marked. Plymouth Colony is shown to the south.

"revealed to," but few simple Puritan women would dare think they merited such notice. Bartholomew did not reply to Anne in London, but his reports of their conversation were recorded much later in Massachusetts.

A 1730 engraving presents a view of Boston 100 years after the capital's founding. When Anne arrived, the town was little more than a collection of small buildings clustered around the harbor.

Exactly one year after the *Griffin* bore Cotton and his two devoted parishioners, Leverett and Hough, to the new colony, it carried more of Cotton's former congregation to join him across the ocean. The Hutchinson family, along with approximately 90 other passengers and 50 officers and seamen, spent 2 months at sea. Conditions on the ship were crowded and unsanitary; the 100 head of cattle in the hold added to the stench. Still days of baking sun alternated with wind and rainstorms. Winthrop wrote of appalling scenes of his own passage four years earlier: "Our landmen [sailors] were very nasty and slovenly . . . where they lodged, was so beastly and noisome with their victuals

and beastliness, as would much endanger the health of the ship." He described one day when "it grew a very great tempest all the night with fierce showers of rain intermixed, and very cold. . . . The sea raged and tossed us exceedingly. . . . A maid-servant in the ship, being stomach-sick . . . near killed herself." Arguments were not uncommon as passengers and crew attempted to maintain an even temper. Anne's passage was marked by a particularly vicious disagreement.

On board the *Griffin* was the Reverend Zechariah Symmes, who had decided that Anne "did slight the ministers of the word of God." His accusation was provoked by her obvious dislike of him and his five-hour sermons. She exclaimed that upon reaching their destination she would prove his teaching was full of errors and proceeded to disregard him for the remainder of the voyage. She began to lecture and meet with women, as she had done in Alford. Some of the men muttered at her boldness.

Symmes then threatened that he would report her activities to the authorities as soon as they landed. He hoped to silence her, but Anne's voice only grew stronger. Before almost all the passengers, she professed that it had been revealed to her that they would reach Boston in the next three weeks. She asked the minister what he would say if this did happen. He scoffed at her until the prediction proved accurate. Immediately upon landing he repeated the tale to Boston church authorities and added other criticisms of his troublesome shipmate.

The *Griffin* docked in Boston in the Massachusetts Bay Colony on September 18, 1634. Anne observed the town that lay before her and found that the pamphlets she had read so eagerly were correct. The town spread out over a small peninsula, but most of the

Puritans carry their scant belongings onshore to their new home. The rigors of the voyage permitted passengers to bring only essential items.

houses, the marketplace, and the meetinghouse were clustered around the spacious harbor on its eastern side. Beyond rose a few hills traced with twisting paths to garden plots and green pastures. Although the town looked no bigger than Alford, it was the commercial, political, and religious hub of the rapidly growing colony—and beset with the troubles that quick expansion brings. Anne was to discover that Boston was not quite the Puritan utopia she sought.

Settlers found the first years of the Massachusetts Bay Colony harsh. Natural disasters, unfriendly Native Americans, and pressure from the king and archbishop in old England imperiled the colony's existence from without; its governors maintained strict discipline to protect the settlement from dissension within. Punishments included public ridicule in the stocks.

FIVE

Puritan Colonist

The moment the *Griffin* docked Anne and William Hutchinson set to work establishing themselves in their new home. One of the first orders of business was joining the First Church of Boston. Six weeks after landing, William applied and was readily admitted, but Symmes, accompanied by William Bartholomew, had promptly reported his dissatisfaction with Anne's shipboard activities to the church authorities. As a result, she was forced to endure a week-long delay after William was admitted while her unorthodox views and behavior were closely scrutinized. She was called to attend a hearing and answer questions about her beliefs from Governor Thomas Dudley, the Reverend Zechariah Symmes, who had been appointed minister of the outlying parish of Charlestown, the Reverend John Wilson, pastor of the Boston congregation, and her former pastor at St. Botolph's, the Reverend John Cotton. Apparently she held up her end of the disputation well, for Dudley recorded that he was "satisfied

that she held nothing different from us." Anne was received into the church November 2, 1634.

The Hutchinsons had arrived in Massachusetts at a time when the colonists were extremely concerned with their relationship to authorities in the mother country. Ensuring that all in the colony held acceptable and harmonious beliefs became more important as intimations of trouble with the king grew louder. The colony was permitted to govern itself, for the entire Massachusetts Bay Company and its charter had been transferred to the colonists. (More commonly the company owners and charter remained in England.) The freemen (citizens) of Boston elected town selectmen and deputies to the General Court to run the municipal government. This privilege was obtained as part of their charter of independence, which could be revoked by the king.

The *Griffin* brought not only new settlers but also a menacing commission Charles I had granted to the An-

John Endecott cut the cross from the king's ensign (flag) in November 1634. The shocking act of defiance caused great concern among members of the General Court.

glican bishops. As Winthrop recorded in his journal, the document named Archbishop Laud as the head of the Lords Commissioners of Plantations (colonies) in General and allowed him and his cohorts "to regulate all plantations, to make laws . . . to remove and punish governors, and to hear and determine all causes [disputes], and inflict all punishments." Alarmed by this language, Winthrop noted the commission was directed "against us, [the Massachusetts Bay Colony] to compel us, by force, to receive a new governor, and the discipline of the church of England." Fortunately for the colonists,

discord grew in England, and Charles I was too busy maintaining order there to enforce his demand and institute his own government in New England. The settlers saw more than ever the need for discipline within their ranks, lest Charles I view his new colonies as additional sources of dissension. Within eight years civil war between the king and Parliament was to break out; before two decades passed Charles I was dethroned and beheaded at the hands of the Puritans in England, but the preceding period was one of increasing pressure from the Crown on the Puritans of New England.

The court faced more evidence of troublemaking just three days after Anne was admitted to the church. They looked aghast upon an act Charles I could have construed as a sign of outright rebellion. John Endecott of Salem, one of the Bay Colony's first settlers, had torn the red cross of St. George from the king's official ensign, charging that it was an emblem of Catholicism. Defacing the flag of the king was so serious a crime that the General Court called witnesses to appear at its next meeting in March, when they could proceed with a full enquiry.

For the next several weeks, the Hutchinsons worked hard at settling in. Winthrop notes in his journal that the autumn of 1634 was hot and dry, which gave William ample opportunity to arrange shelter for the 15 people in his household. He appears to have been able to provide for them well. From his inheritance and business profits, William had amassed a considerable amount of money. His economic status entitled him to be called "Mr." rather than "Goodman" (as members of the lower class were addressed), and Anne was known as "Mistress Hutchinson." Their standing in the community is attested to by the parcel of land the municipality granted them. Their half-acre lot on the corner of Sentry Street and High Street was in the best section of town, conveniently across the street from the town spring and diagonally opposite the home of former governor Winthrop and his wife, Margaret. Two nearby buildings housed the well-respected households of John and Mary

An engraving depicts two well-off members of the Massachusetts Bay Colony in typical attire. The Puritans stressed simplicity in their services as well as in their clothing.

Coggeshall and Atherton and Elizabeth Hough.

Aided by hired hands, William set to work building a commodious two-story wooden home. Around a large brick chimney that opened into fireplaces in several rooms, there was a spacious parlor, a kitchen, and several bedrooms and storage chambers on the second floor. A lean-to built against a ground-floor wall provided William and his elder sons with an area to display their textiles and transact business. The bedrooms were full, for in addition to Anne, William, and their 11 children,

William housed 2 unmarried female cousins of his own, Anne and Frances Freiston.

Anne enjoyed her new life and her new surroundings. The stern, devout Reverend Wilson had returned to England to coax his strong-minded wife, Elizabeth, to join him in the New World. She had adamantly refused to make the journey for the past four years. In his absence the Reverend John Cotton took over sole responsibility for the affairs of the First Church of Boston. Once again, Anne could listen to his eloquent, uplifting sermons. But in her new home she did not have to travel days before she could hear his message. She had only to take a 15-minute stroll down High Street to the meetinghouse, a square wooden building near Bendall's Dock, the main facility for ships in the harbor.

The Hutchinsons relished the colony's rejection of any trappings of the hated Church of England. Boston's church, unlike those back in England, had no lofty spires and no ivy clinging to its stones. It was plain, with mud-chinked wooden walls and a grass-thatched roof. Sunday was soberly referred to as the Lord's Day or the Sabbath, and the names of Anglican feast days were no longer used. The Puritans of Boston stopped celebrating at Christmas, and they stripped their marriage ceremony of religious over-tones. Marriages were no longer performed by ministers in a church; instead, special officials or magistrates presided over marriages in a civil ceremony.

Anne unpacked her belongings, arranging the few pieces of furniture, valued heirlooms and knickknacks, and packets of medicinal herbs she had carried on the trip across the Atlantic. She began to investigate her unfamiliar new home. Anne had time in which to do so because for the first time in many years she was not pregnant, even though Susanna, her 14th child, was no more than a year old. In addition, because they lived in the center of town rather than the countryside, she could purchase more of the family's food at the market. She no longer spent hours preparing time-consuming items such as butter and cheese herself. She spent an increasing amount of time pondering the Bible, waiting for the Holy Spirit to reveal the meaning of puzzling passages to her. Although she had missed Cotton's preaching in England, once again his sermons on the grace of God within the saved inspired her to study and renewed her faith in grace rather than works.

Nevertheless, feeding 15 adults and children in New England was not an easy job. Livestock of any kind were rare, and in the absence of roast beef and mutton, the colonists ate wild game. Familiar grains such as barley, oats, and wheat did not grow abundantly, and the colonists owed much to the Native Americans who taught them to grow corn. No flour meant little bread and no beer; instead, Bostonians learned to cook cornmeal, mussels, clams, lobster, beans, and squash and to drink the abundant fresh water. Because no sugar maples grew in the

Anne enjoyed the large home that William built for his family. The house included a spacious kitchen that Anne equipped with the cooking utensils she had carried from England. A 20th-century reconstruction provides modern viewers with an idea of what such a kitchen was like.

old country, the settlers knew nothing of maple syrup, but when Native Americans introduced them to the sweetener tapped from the trees, housewives were delighted and quickly added it to their recipes. Anne—intelligent, energetic, and inquiring—adapted well to these changes. Soon she even grew adept at using the herbs of the New World to soothe the ills of her fellow Bostonians. She never failed to care for her neighbors, with whom she quickly became popular during the bitterly cold winter of 1634–35.

William also found Boston much to his liking. In March 1635, the General Court met again, and William and his sons Richard and Francis took the oath of freemen. Two months later at the next meeting and annual election in May 1635, neither John Winthrop nor Thomas Dudley were reinstated as governor. Instead, John Haynes, an extremely wealthy man who had arrived in Boston only two years earlier, was elected. His deputy governor was Richard Bellingham, a lawyer who had arrived only the previous year. At the same time, Endecott was formally censured for defacing the ensign and forbidden to hold office for one year, and William Hutchinson was elected as a deputy to the General Court. For the next year and a half, he served as deputy, then became an appraiser and magistrate called to settle small cases in the courts. In the spring of 1636, the freemen of Boston elected him as one of their selectmen and reelected him to that post for the next four half-year terms.

Anne had merely to look at her own husband and church to see that both the political and the religious organization of the colony was quite different from that of England. Abhorring the pomp of the Anglican church and the domination of nobles, the Puritans labored in the wilderness to create a new way of life. The common English people might spend a lifetime with never a sight of their ruler, the king; the goodmen and goodwomen of Boston could see their governor nearly every day. That governor did not pass his post on to his son, but like every other officeholder was subject to replacement at the voters' command in each annual May election.

Each community had its own church under a covenant that the congregants themselves had formulated. Congregants also chose their church members, and each church took care of individual disciplinary problems. They did not wait for pronouncements from the bishops of the Church of England and often did not listen to the ones they received.

Yet the colony was not a democracy, and the Puritan church had vast influence over the life of every member of the settlement. Puritans had absolutely no tolerance for religious dissent. In the eyes of Winthrop and many other leaders, order was best maintained by rigid orthodoxy—allowing any individual to challenge that divinely inspired order could destroy the entire fragile enterprise. They were determined to keep Massachusetts Bay independent of religious or political interference from England—although they strenuously denied they were Separatists. In the attempt to make the powers across the ocean think all was well and quiet in the colony, the ministers and magistrates ruthlessly suppressed any challenge to uniformity or authority. They even enacted a dress code that forbade the wearing of jewelry, handsome fabrics, detailed embroideries, and long hair. In their churches, the women entered and left by one door, the men by another, and each sat on their own side, arranged by social standing, which continued to play a prominent role in Massachusetts Bay. Not every man was a freeman worthy of the right to vote and hold office. Only members of the church could hold the rights of citizenship.

Although men and women were segregated in church and the idea of a woman voting was unthinkable, Anne found that women were better treated than in England. Laws existed forbidding a husband from beating his wife. Jail and heavy fines awaited transgressors. As she stopped and chatted at the spring she was pleased to learn that before her arrival Cotton had succeeded in squelching a proposal to force women to wear veils. Even severe John Winthrop, governor at the time, proclaimed the idea preposterous.

During her visits to neighbors, Anne probably heard many tales about political squabbles and the hard times the founding families endured. She found her competence at folk medicine and midwifery even more valuable than in England, for the unfamiliar and some-

A German woodcut shows a midwife (left) at work. Until late in the 19th century, births were attended not by doctors in hospitals but by midwives at home. Anne's expertise as a midwife made her exceedingly popular among the women of Boston.

times scanty diet and the harsh weather contributed to many illnesses. Only three other people in the colony ministered at all knowledgeably to the ill and the pregnant in 1634. The well-respected Thomas Oliver was a surgeon but his duties as town selectman occupied much of his time. A barber-surgeon named William Dinely traveled about cutting hair and pulling teeth, and Jane Hawkins, a simple, eccentric woman who had been denied

*A young Puritan woman spins thread. Able performance of such a
task was expected of women, and Anne competently ran her own
household. She also led well-attended lectures and discussions about
religion in her parlor, taking on a most unusual role for a woman.*

membership in the church, aided at births. The women of the colony, many of them separated from mothers, grandmothers, older sisters, and aunts to advise them, eagerly welcomed Anne's skill and experience and kept her very busy.

Anne was so occupied with her children, her neighbors, her study of the Bible, and her churchgoing that she had no time to attend the afternoon prayer meetings where many women gathered. An acquaintance told her that local gossips looked askance at her absence. Because she had been so well schooled by her father and spent so much time on her own contemplating Scripture, Anne felt qualified to begin holding assemblies for women in her own home. The practice began slowly, as half a dozen women met once a week in the Hutchinsons' large parlor. Winthrop, her closest neighbor, barely took notice. Cotton encouraged the meetings, perhaps flattered that Anne's sole purpose was to repeat his sermons and discuss them with women unable to attend Lord's Day services. As the assemblies grew, Anne began explaining Cotton's sermons and expanding on them. Though she did not differ significantly from him, she stressed the covenant of grace even more than he did. She even more firmly believed in her ability to communicate directly with God through careful reading and interpretation of the Scriptures.

For several months, the colony's officials looked on her meetings with approval, although almost every woman in Boston had begun to attend on a regular basis. Anne's parlor had become a place where women could go for comfort and support. Adjusting to harsh colonial life, separated from family and friends, these hardworking women were sometimes lonely and scared. Meeting their neighbors and thoughtfully discussing the religion they shared and the single weekly sermon they all heard was a welcome break.

Throughout the summer of 1635, William occupied himself with his business and the affairs of the town; Anne, at the age of 44 and pregnant for the 15th time, continued ministering to her neighbors at their bedside and in her parlor. More serious concerns troubled the General Court. At the July meeting of this body, the magistrates summoned Roger Williams, the minister of Salem, an outlying community, to answer grave charges. His sermons urging complete separation from the Church of England had worried the colony's leaders, for they differed from the course the founders had chosen to pursue. Many felt his preaching had inspired Endecott to commit his outrageous assault on the king's emblem. On numerous matters, ranging from whether prayers should be said after meals to whether the king of England even had the right to grant the land of Native Americans to British subjects, Williams's unorthodox opinions enraged the court. As Winthrop records in his journal, the court requested advice from the ministers. Men of the cloth gravely consulted each other and noted, "A church might run into heresy, apos-

The original charter of Massachusetts gave the colony's inhabitants the power to govern themselves. Charles I repeatedly threatened to send a royal governor of his own choosing in place of the colonists' annually elected executive, but troubled affairs in England prevented him from doing so.

tacy, or tyranny . . . [if] the civil magistrate could not intermeddle." They concluded, "He who should obstinately maintain such opinions . . . were to be removed, and that the other churches ought to request the magistrates so to do." The subtle nuances of the relationship between church and state in Puritan New England were revealed by this conclusion. Ministers were not magistrates, but the duties of magistrates apparently included enforcing religious conformity. Williams and his Salem congregation, who had stubbornly promoted him in the face of official displeasure, were commanded to think about their errors and either apologize or face a civil sentence at the next meeting of the General Court. Anne must have heard of the turmoil but probably never suspected how closely such an issue would affect her.

William Hutchinson followed the progress of the troublesome cleric, too, just as he would have noticed any important event in the colony. The merchants of Boston kept up with the latest news from the General Court, for the deputies exercised considerable influence on commerce. Since the colony's founding, demand for goods had outstripped supply. As the numbers of settlers grew, they needed more metal tools, household utensils, livestock, cloth, rope, and other necessities. All these commodities were imported and so were available in limited quantities. Shipmasters and merchants wealthy enough to buy entire shiploads did so and retailed the highly desired cargoes at what many inhabitants considered exorbitant prices. The court acted quickly to impose price controls. The clergy supported these controls, for they did not deem unscrupulous business dealings a mark of the saved. The General Court experimented with a number of unsuccessful schemes of price regulation and controls.

By September 1635, the businessmen of Boston defied the government by forming their own committee in an effort to reconcile their needs for a profit with the governor's demand for regulation. The committee consisted of three prominent businessmen: William Brenton, William Colburn, and William Hutchinson. Unfortunately, their attempt could not solve the problem either.

Some of these businessmen learned of Anne's meetings and her stress on the covenant of grace by conversing with the women of the colony. The established clergy frowned upon the works of merchants, and the businessmen found Anne's deemphasis of works attractive. In addition, she was a persuasive and charismatic speaker, and her knowledge of Scripture was extensive. Anne's meetings were soon packed with eager followers.

Anne's talents and spirit made her an exceptional woman. However, in the 17th century, women did not participate in politics or religion. Even though a wife might voice opinions in her own home and have the ear of her husband, outside that environment a woman was expected to remain silent. Anne certainly did not fill the conventional role. On October 6, 1635, two large ships from England, the *Defence* and the *Abigail*, docked in Boston Harbor. On board were several men who would make Anne's days in the Massachusetts Bay Colony even more controversial.

The Reverend John Cotton, an eminent theologian, was driven from England by Archbishop Laud for preaching Puritan doctrines. His ideas about the covenant of grace inspired Anne Hutchinson, and she followed him to Massachusetts, where he was held in high esteem.

SIX

"Doubtful Disputations"

Among the more than 200 travelers disembarking from the *Defence* and *Abigail* were the Reverend John Wilson, pastor of the First Church of Boston, the Reverend Hugh Peter, who had been head of a Puritan church in Holland, and Sir Henry Vane. Wilson had finally persuaded his wife to accompany him to the New World and enthusiastically returned to preaching. Peter almost immediately set to work helping the colonists found a fishing industry. Vane was a 22-year-old aristocrat, the son of the king's comptroller. His father had trained him in diplomacy to prepare for a career at court, but to his father's dismay the young man embraced Puritan doctrines and refused to accept the Church of England. Opposed by his father, but encouraged by the king, Vane traveled to join the Puritans in New England, who welcomed him wholeheartedly. The community hoped that Vane could give them more direct access to the king, for his father sat on the king's Privy Council (a group of close advisers) and might convince the king to stop threatening to rescind the original charter.

That same October the General Court expelled Roger Williams from the church and colony for his unorthodox views, demanding that he leave their jurisdiction within six weeks. He traveled south into the wilderness and founded the town of Providence and the colony of Rhode Island, where he encouraged religious toleration. A few weeks later, on November 1, 1635, Henry Vane was admitted to the Boston church. Having dispensed with the troublesome Williams, the colony's leaders were anxious to resolve other divisive issues.

Three months after Vane arrived, he was greatly honored by an invitation to preside over a panel called to settle a long-standing dispute between Winthrop and Dudley. The two men disagreed on a number of issues of public

Roger Williams was banished from Boston in 1635 for holding religious views at variance with the established church. In January 1636, the General Court sent officers to take custody of him and force him to return to England, but he eluded them and traveled south during the severe winter months. He established the colony of Rhode Island, where he encouraged religious toleration.

policy, but the January meeting was held specifically to judge opposing approaches to dispensing justice in the colony. Winthrop favored intelligent leniency; former governor Dudley believed in stern discipline. After listening to arguments from both sides, the panel decided that a newly founded colony needed strict discipline to en-

sure the safety of each individual, the church, and the state. Immediately, Winthrop admitted that he had been overly lenient in the past and would not repeat the mistake in the future. Winthrop would long remember this chastisement.

The following spring, in March 1636, the Hutchinsons' son Zuriel was baptized, and as quickly as Anne had retired from society, she returned. The long winter months and the difficulties of pregnancy in middle age had limited Anne's activities, but she spent the time thinking even more deeply about religion and closely studying the Bible. She also listened to Wilson's Lord's Day sermons with great displeasure. While the irascible Wilson had been in England, Anne had become accustomed to listening to Cotton's enlightening sermons. Wilson's style was much different. He was not eloquent, and John Cotton's prominent grandson, Cotton Mather, recorded in his history of the New England church, *Magnalia Christi Americana*, that Wilson "preached more after the primitive manner . . . chiefly in exhortations and admonitions." Anne heard him urge his congregation to labor to perform works according to the Scriptures to show they were saved. Her dislike for Wilson and his staid, stuffy sermons led her to compare them to Cotton's sermons. She concluded that Wilson preached a covenant of works, for he stressed public evidence of morality and made little of a believer's knowledge of the grace of the Holy Spirit within.

Again she presided over her well-attended assemblies, which had been curtailed during the latter part of her pregnancy. One fateful difference in her discussions soon became apparent. She began comparing Cotton's sermons to Wilson's and made clear her distaste for the latter's covenant of works. She boldly pointed out what she considered to be Wilson's defects, and many who gathered in her parlor agreed with her assessment. One of Wilson's sermons so incensed her that she stood up and led her followers out of church.

Among the audience at her meetings, which she held twice a week, were increasing numbers of businessmen—and Henry Vane. The usual attendees included her neighbors on three sides, the Coggeshalls, the Houghs, and Samuel Cole, an innkeeper, along with his wife, Anne. Some had been neighbors in Alford: Thomas and William Wardall and Thomas Marshall, who ran the ferry from Boston to Newtown, a community on the mainland, across the bay from the peninsula of Boston. William and Mary Dyer were enthusiastic listeners, traveling from a more distant section called South Cove, as were William and Margery Colburn, who came from an area called Boston Neck, the narrow strip of land connecting Boston to the mainland. William Coddington, probably the wealthiest man in Boston, attended regularly, as did Edward Bendall, the owner of Bendall's Dock, and the merchants William Brenton and Robert Harding. Many held offices in the colony; several served as representatives to the General

Sir Henry Vane the Younger arrived in Boston in November 1635 and was elected to the governorship the following May. He presided over one of the most turbulent years of the colony's early history, but he is best known for his statesmanship during the English civil war. Two years after the restoration of the monarchy in England in 1660, he was executed.

Court, and 12 were continually re-elected as selectmen. Anne counted most of the political and economic elite of Boston among her supporters, except for Winthrop, Bellingham, and Dudley.

The beginning of the summer of 1636 brought excellent news for Anne. In May, Henry Vane was elected governor of the colony. That same month, Anne's brother-in-law John Wheelwright and his wife, Mary, arrived in Boston. When Cotton had been too ill

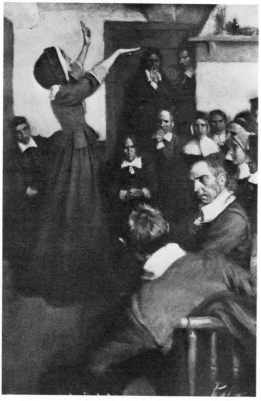

An early-20th-century artist's rendering of Anne preaching at her house shows a number of men in attendance. Anne attracted some of the wealthiest and most powerful merchants in Boston to her meetings, which increased Winthrop's fear of her faction.

she assured her followers, clearly taught a covenant of grace. Vane agreed with her and expressed his support by faithfully attending her meetings.

Over the summer, Anne's assemblies grew in size. Former selectmen, deputies, wealthy merchants, a minister, the current governor, and many women attended her meetings. The existence of such a sizable body of supporters finally alarmed Wilson, who had so far approved of Anne's activities. When he spoke with one of her followers, he learned that Anne directly criticized his ministry and her religious views varied greatly from those held by orthodox ministers. As Anne had expanded her speeches praising the doctrine of free grace, she had arrived at a position much further from Cotton than even she realized. Wilson did not attack her at once but spoke more forcefully on Sundays about how necessary it was for believers to show their salvation by the works they performed rather than relying on their own sense of an indwelling Holy Spirit.

Winthrop was also alarmed by the presence of any faction within the colony. He began to question the purpose of Anne's meetings and worried that she might be causing trouble. His suspicions were strengthened by the prejudices of the era. Anne made her way into women's lives easily, for she was an excellent midwife and nurse whose patients almost always felt better, and the mothers and newborn infants she cared for generally grew strong and healthy. Like many people of the time, Winthrop viewed midwifery with sus-

to preach in England, she had found solace in the sermons of Wheelwright. Anne welcomed the arrival of a minister who stressed the covenant of grace as she thought a minister should. Dissatisfied with Wilson, she traveled around the various churches in the colony and was aghast to discover that all seemed to preach a covenant of works. Only Cotton and Wheelwright,

One of Winthrop's many letters to his wife, Margaret. He expressed himself more freely in his frequent notes to her than in his official pronouncements and journals, and several letters reveal his personal concern for her well-being. Others give glimpses of the despair he felt over the colony's troubles.

picion. Very little was known about medicine, pregnancy, and childbirth, and all too often, ignorance bred fear and distrust. Although Anne's knowledge of these little-understood mysteries may have disturbed Winthrop, she upset him even more when she stepped into the political arena. In his journal, he recorded his dislike of women "who meddle in such things as are proper for men, whose minds are stronger." After having been reprimanded for leniency the previous January, he had no intention of tolerating anyone who troubled the peace of the colony, particularly a woman.

Knowing that Anne valued Cotton's opinions highly, Wilson and Winthrop suggested he speak with her at his first opportunity. He did meet with her and several of her adherents, attempting to point out how their views were in error and not his own at all. They denied they held unorthodox, or heretical, opinions. Wilson and Winthrop then convinced Cotton to send spies to her meetings, but the women of his church he sent to attend her assemblies reported that Anne said nothing to warrant alarm.

By the fall of 1636, Anne's following had become a powerful faction, supported by Governor Vane and the Reverend John Wheelwright. Winthrop continued to worry, convinced of Anne's "dangerous errors." That summer some of the Native Americans in the area, the Pequot tribe, had murdered a trader who infringed on their land rights. Endecott had led a bloody expedition against them but merely stirred up more trouble. Winthrop thought that in the face of threats such as this the colony could not afford to be torn apart by internal divisions. As deputy governor to Vane, however, there was little he could do.

Wilson had his own problems as he struggled to hold the First Church of Boston together. In October 1637, Anne and her staunch adherents proposed that John Wheelwright be named assistant teacher in Wilson's Boston congregation. Confident that Wheelwright would reinforce the teachings of Cotton, they planned to ease Wilson out of his position as pastor and replace him with Cotton, aided by Wheelwright as teacher. Their bold move threw both church and state into an uproar.

The debate over Wheelwright's appointment began during a church service in late October. Winthrop rose to do battle. He contended that the church had able ministers whom the congregation already knew. In his journal, he recorded his claim that Wheelwright "seemed to dissent in judgment," or hold opinions not approved by all. Governor Vane impulsively stood to say that Cotton himself approved Wheelwright's doctrine. Cotton, always conciliatory, managed to support both sides. Though Winthrop was outnumbered, he refused to support the appointment of Wheelwright, maintaining that the argument they had engaged in proved Wheelwright "was apt to raise doubtful disputations." Because they could not agree unanimously, Winthrop effectively won. Wilson was to remain as minister with Cotton as teacher at Boston, and Wheelwright was given an appointment as minister at Mount Wollaston, a small community about 10 miles from Boston, where Anne's husband and many of her supporters, including William Coddington, owned farms and other property. Though the congregation there might be congenial to Wheelwright, the distance made it a tough day's travel for Bostonians who desired to attend his church services.

Winter began and the controversy grew. Letters flew back and forth among Winthrop, Cotton, and Vane. The young governor steadfastly supported Anne and claimed the person of the Holy Spirit dwelled in believers; Winthrop replied that the *person* of the Holy Spirit was never discussed in Scripture. By this point the theological arguments had became tortuously involved and abstruse, confusing many members of the congregation—and several later commentators on the affair as well. One eminent 19th-century historian, Charles Francis Adams, remarked in his book about the controversy, "Not only were the points obscure, but the discussion was carried on in a jargon which has become unintelligible." What remains clear is the depth of the division between Vane, Wheelwright, and Anne's adherents on one side and Winthrop, Wilson, and strictly orthodox ministers from nearby communities on the other.

At last the pressure and criticism from Winthrop and his colleagues became too intense for the 23-year-old Vane. He announced that news from England forced him to return to attend to personal matters there. Winthrop happily arranged a session of the General Court in early December to accept his resignation. When one assistant to the court pleaded with him to stay, Vane broke down crying. He confessed, as Winthrop notes, that he feared the "danger . . . of God's judgments to come upon us for these differences and dissensions, which he saw amongst us, and the scandalous imputations [accusations of misbehavior] brought upon himself, as if he should be the cause of all." The deputies to the court refused to accept his resignation, some because they valued his support of Anne, others because they feared he would report their disorganization and dissensions to the king. After the people of Boston sent him a written plea to remain with them, Vane was persuaded to stay in office until his term ended in May 1637.

Soon after, ministers who had come to Boston from surrounding settlements to discuss the dissension in the Boston church met and sent a letter to Cotton, asking him to explain exactly how his doctrines differed from theirs. Meanwhile, Vane presided over a meeting of ministers called to express their views about the turmoil to the court. The Reverend Hugh Peter seized the floor and upbraided the young governor, claiming that until Vane arrived there had been no problems in the New England churches. Wilson took the opportunity to speak his mind next. He began by condemning the "new opinions risen up amongst us" and embarked on a bitter speech chastising

Puritans journey to services in the cold. On January 20, 1637, the colonists observed a fast day to consider their differences and bring harmony to their church, but John Wheelwright's sermon that day

*only fueled more controversy. As Winthrop observed of the period,
"Every occasion increased the contention, and caused great alienation
of minds."*

certain members of the Boston church—Anne and her followers. He also insinuated that Cotton was partly responsible for the trouble. His heated, blunt speaking infuriated Cotton and many others present. Several church members visited him at home and asked him exactly what he had implied in his speech before the court. They wondered if he had dared attack members of his own church outright. Wilson denied the charges, but on December 31, 1636, he appeared before his congregation to answer questions from all of them. Vane mercilessly criticized him, and other parishioners became so incensed that they called for a vote of censure (formal condemnation), which would have led to his expulsion from the church. Cotton intervened to prevent such a drastic step, but the damage had been done. Wilson became an even more bitter opponent of Anne and her followers, who had embarrassed him so profoundly in his own church.

Amid the turmoil, at Winthrop and Wilson's suggestion, Cotton invited Anne to his house for questioning by several ministers. She was greeted by the gentle face of her highly esteemed minister, Cotton; her brother-in-law and advocate, Wheelwright; the conservative and vociferous Hugh Peter; and four other stern inquisitors. Peter spoke for the ministers and informed her she had been summoned because of reports that she had condemned their ministry. He asked her why she insisted that only Cotton and Wheelwright were able ministers and demanded to know why she failed to see that the others

taught correctly. Again and again, Anne tried to explain that they did not preach the covenant of grace as well as Cotton and Wheelwright did. Displaying a considerable mastery of Scripture and points of doctrine, she angered several ministers and impressed others. Unfortunately, she wound up claiming that most clergy could not preach correctly even if they wished to, for they were not "sealed" ministers. The debate foundered as the ministers confused themselves with various theological terms, but despite their differences, the meeting ended when Anne seemed to satisfy them with her answers.

On January 20, 1637, a general fast day was observed in an attempt to bring harmony to the colony. Winthrop and the other ministers had failed to pressure Cotton into moving away from Anne, despite another round of copious letter writing. During the fast day, Wheelwright delivered a sermon that infuriated Winthrop and Wilson. Wilson interpreted the sermon as an indictment of his own preaching; Winthrop deemed it a call for civil war.

Two months later, the General Court, advised by a council of ministers, examined Wheelwright's inflammatory fast day sermon. A few weeks previously, the court had passed brutal legislation levying harsh fines on businessmen accused of overcharging for imported goods. The court also authorized the search of incoming ships and warehouses without a warrant. Both actions alienated the businessmen of Boston. Many of Anne's adherents deeply resented Wilson's attacks on

Anne's and their own beliefs. As merchants, they resented the financial penalties imposed by the General Court as well. William Hutchinson, among many others, protested. Hutchinson proceeded to resign his post as one of the three deputies from Boston to the General Court and left his appointment as appraiser for the courts.

When the General Court was prepared to address Wheelwright's sermon, they summoned him and he presented the text of his speech. The next day the court received a petition signed by most of the members of the Boston church requesting that their proceedings be held in public, a plea that Winthrop labeled presumptuous and promptly disregarded. Although the petition was signed only by male church members, it is highly probable that Anne wrote it. After days of stormy public and private deliberations, despite the protests of Governor Vane, one of the most avid supporters of Hutchinson and her beliefs, the court found Wheelwright "guilty of sedition and also of contempt" but postponed his sentencing until after the upcoming May gubernatorial election, for opposition to the verdict was strong. As Winthrop records, "Much heat of contention was [at] this court between the opposite parties." The conservative elements, including Winthrop and Wilson, wanted to place more of their candidates on the court in May to en-

sure that stern punishment would be meted out to Wheelwright. In March, the beleaguered minister could still count on firm support from those of Anne's followers who sat on the court. To further benefit the conservative candidates from outlying districts, Winthrop, with the aid of Endecott, managed to move the election from Boston to Newtown, farther from Hutchinson's supporters and closer to Winthrop's. Vane protested and tried to block the vote, but his youth and inexperience made him no match for the politically astute Winthrop, who had his ally Endecott carry the motion.

Men from Charlestown, Ipswich, Roxbury, Newbury, and Salem joined 57 Boston freemen in signing a statement protesting Wheelwright's conviction. William Aspinwall drafted the petition, and although Anne and her female followers could not sign it, nearly all the men who supported her did. The document, with a total of 74 signatures, was practically a role call of her adherents. No outcry greeted this remonstrance (as the signatories termed it), but eventually it loomed large in Boston affairs. The stage was set for the election of 1637. Boston had been split in two. Anne's apprehension grew after Wheelwright's conviction, but she continued to hold meetings and minister to the sick. Her inexhaustible energy and indomitable spirit were obvious. Her fate was not.

A 19th-century engraving depicts a scene at the General Court. Although the artist misrepresented the appearance of the building, he portrayed the emotional temper of Anne's trial in November 1637, during which several heated discussions and outbursts erupted.

SEVEN

"Unfit for Our Society"

May 17, 1637, was warm and sunny. Around a large oak tree on the grassy field of Newtown Common, the men of the Massachusetts Bay Colony gathered to elect their governor for the coming year. As had been the custom in England, the election was held in the open air. Since March, members of the contending factions in the colony had eagerly conferred among themselves about the election, and the hum of discussions rose from the green. Each side of the theological dispute had chosen their candidate: Anne and her followers supported Henry Vane's reelection; Wilson, Endecott, and the conservatives supported Winthrop. Anne's name disappears from the public chronicles at this point because women had no political identity—they could neither vote nor hold office. But her fate was tied to that of Vane, the champion of the Hutchinsonians; his success or failure was the key to her followers' fortune.

Winthrop's success at moving the election proved crucial to its outcome. In later years travel from Boston to Newtown (now Cambridge) became easier, but in 1637 the distance was great. Any Bostonian journeying to Newtown faced a boat trip or a long overland route that circled south and west around the bay. Although all voters were proportionately represented by deputies, freemen from Roxbury, Watertown, Charlestown, Salem, and other outlying communities had a less difficult trip to the election and outnumbered Bostonians there. Many of these residents of other settlements felt that members of the Boston church were troublemakers. Boston merchants had not only enriched themselves at the expense of the rest of the colony but also recently snubbed them. A few weeks before the election the Boston congregation's ministers and governor had insulted the congregation of Concord. Vane, Wheelright, Cotton, and two elders of the church, Thomas Leverett and Thomas Oliver, refused an invitation to attend the ordination of the Reverend Peter Bulkley as teacher and a Mr. Jones as pastor at Concord, for as Winthrop notes, "they accounted these as legal preachers [supporters of the covenant of works]." The day was bright and calm, but the crowd was tense and resentful.

The freemen of outlying towns chatted with one another, perhaps muttering over the troubles in Boston. At one o'clock in the afternoon, as voting was to begin, a man suddenly spoke up, demanding to read a petition from Boston appealing the March judgment against Wheelwright. Vane agreed it should be read; Winthrop was determined it should not. He shouted that the meeting was a Court of Elections and an appeal had no place. Vane insisted on hearing it, and voices rose as Bostonians pressed their point. Wilson, despite his age and solemn demeanor, actually climbed into the branches of the oak tree and bellowed down at the noisy throng. By this point members of the crowd had begun shoving and punching each other, but at the sight of Wilson in the tree, the tumult subsided and cries of "Elections! Elections!" arose. Winthrop called for a simple majority vote on whether to read the appeal or proceed to vote. His relocation of the election proved telling at last, for the Bostonians were outnumbered. More than half of those present decided it was time to vote.

The Boston candidates suffered a rout at the polls. Vane was soundly defeated.

William Coddington and Atherton Hough, who belonged to Wheelwright's congregation at Mount Wollaston and who ran with Vane for positions as deputy and magistrate, also lost. Winthrop became governor; Dudley, deputy governor. Thomas Leverett and Israel Stoughton were chosen as assistants, and Wilson was elected a member of the standing council for life. Once again, the Massachusetts Bay Colony would be run by the same two men who had overseen its founding and first three years of existence.

The defeated party made its displeasure known at once. The honor guard that had attended Vane came from Boston, and these four men (one of whom was a brother-in-law of Anne's, Edward Hutchinson) refused to march with Winthrop. Instead they cast their halberds (ceremonial weapons) aside in disgust and left him to walk alone. In addition, the Bostonians, wary of the outcome, had refused to elect deputies to the General Court until after the gubernatorial election. Their fears proved justified, so they immediately proposed their defeated slate of candidates: Vane, Coddington, and Hough. This choice reaffirmed the strength of Anne's support, for all three were staunch disciples of hers. Winthrop refused to accept this slap at the court that had just driven Vane and Coddington from office. He seized on a flimsy pretext to nullify the Bostonians' choice—two freemen of Boston had not been informed of the election. Undaunted, Anne's supporters knocked on the door of every freeman in Boston and speedily reelected the Hutchinson supporters to the court. Winthrop had no choice but to accept them.

The Massachusetts General Court of 1637 was composed of 43 members. The colonists as a whole chose 11 magistrates, and each of the 14 towns that made up Massachusetts Bay elected their own deputies, who numbered 32 in all. Although almost all of Boston supported Anne, there were only 3 Boston representatives on the court. The court's first order of business was to call Wheelwright before them. They admonished him to consider his errors and apologize for or retract his fast day sermon. The fiery minister, thoroughly tired of appearing before the narrow-minded magistrates, replied that if he were, in fact, guilty of sedition he should be put to death. If the court was going to proceed against him he would take his appeal to the king. The court erupted, and Winthrop records the chamber was filled with "their tumultuous course, and divers[e] insolent speeches." It was decided to postpone final judgment until the August session. Even more serious business was at hand.

Conflict with the Native Americans had grown over the winter. One month earlier a special session of court had imposed new taxes to raise funds for equipping 160 men to do battle with the Pequots in the neighboring colony of Connecticut. Nine days after Winthrop took office, the Pequot War broke out in earnest, and the fighting raged from May 26 to July 28, 1637. Outnumbered but better armed, the colonists savagely defeated the Pequots in a "divine slaughter," according to one clergyman. But Bostonians still seethed at their defeat at the polls, and the selection of Wilson as chaplain of the expedition enraged them further. Boston freemen balked at serving with a minister who taught a covenant of works. Anne's followers flatly refused to send money, men, or supplies.

Anne courageously continued to lead her assemblies. Her followers persisted in vexing Winthrop. Vane and Coddington, who formerly had sat in places of honor among the magistrates during religious services, pointedly marched into the church on the Sunday after the election, disdained to sit with Winthrop, and settled in with the lower-ranked deacons, despite the new governor's invitation to resume their old place. For months angry congregants had shouted challenges about points of doctrine and the covenant of works at ministers after sermons; widespread dissatisfaction with the electoral outcome did nothing to silence the obstreperous parishioners.

The court was still convened when news reached Boston that a body of English emigrants from the church of Roger Brierly of Lancashire was at sea, bound for Massachusetts. Brierly was known to look kindly on Familism. Another group was expected from Lincolnshire, including Samuel Hutchinson and several friends of Anne's. The new governor skillfully took advantage of his position to deny Anne these reinforcements. Alarmed by the idea of new arrivals with divisive opinions,

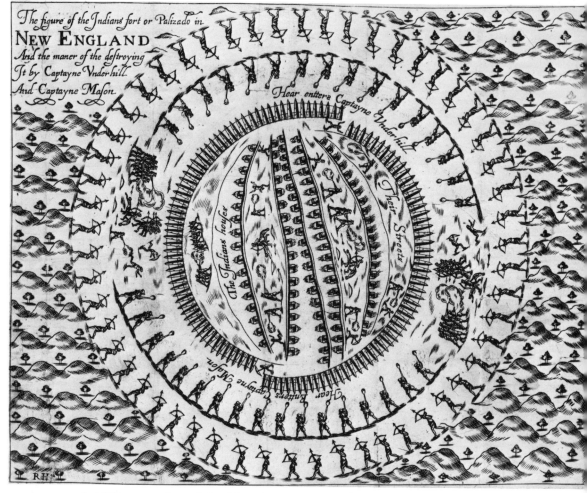

A 1638 engraving of the May 25, 1637, attack on the Pequot fort at Mystic, Connecticut. Captains John Underhill and John Mason led the ruthless and bloody assault, which Winthrop noted resulted in the killing of "two chief sachems, and one hundred and fifty fighting men, and about one hundred and fifty old men, women, and children" among the Pequots. Two colonists died in the raid.

Winthrop directed the court to pass an alien exclusion law. The law, set to expire in one year, mandated that no immigrant could purchase a house or live in any town for more than three weeks without express permission from one member of the governor's council or two magistrates. Because all the magistrates were Winthrop's allies, he could exclude any newcomer who did not take his side.

Twice during the month of June,

ships arrived with orders from the king insisting that his own appointed commissioners should replace locally elected government officials. Charles I claimed that without royal approval no lawful authority existed. The contentious colonists did agree on one major point—the charter would not be rescinded.

Winthrop was beset with problems—the commands from the king, the war with the Pequots, and the contempt of the people of Boston. Still, he had firm control of the government, the support of the ministers, and a solid power base among the 13 other towns in the colony. Perhaps to reassure himself, he set off on a formal visit to three of them—Saugus, Salem, and Ipswich—where he was greeted with enthusiasm and public honors.

No such welcome awaited him at home, however. He returned to Boston during a torrid heat wave that forced him to travel at night. Boston baked that summer; several colonists searching for homesteads succumbed to heat stroke. These new settlers, of whom Winthrop heartily approved, had arrived on the *Hector*, along with Lord Ley, the 19-year-old son of the earl of Marlborough, who intended to stay for a brief visit. Winthrop hastily invited the young man to stay at his own home, but Ley, who seems to have been somewhat shy and retiring, declined. Before long, Vane made friends with his fellow young noble, and together they issued a resounding insult to Winthrop. Anxious to impress any English noble, Winthrop arranged a dinner party at his home to introduce the outstanding men of New England to Lord Ley. Not only did Vane decline the invitation, claiming that his conscience would not permit him to dine with such men, but he also took Lord Ley to dinner himself on Nottle's Island at the home of Mr. Maverick, who had never even bothered to apply for admission to the church of Boston.

About a week later, "Here came over a brother of Mrs. Hutchinson, and some other of Mr. Wheelwright's friends, whom the governor thought not fit to allow . . . among us," Winthrop noted in his journal. The Pequots still threatened, and the new arrivals had just endured the perils of an ocean crossing. Unsurprisingly, Winthrop's decision to deny them sanctuary in the colony was, as he put it, "taken very ill" by the Hutchinsonians.

To reconcile the colonists, Cotton agreed to preach a sermon on harmony. Winthrop, in an attempt to further Cotton's theme of peace, declared the differences between Anne's beliefs and the others far from fatal. To lend credence to this statement, he proposed a religious synod (special meeting or assembly) at Newtown to bring unity to the divided Puritans. Every member of the colony was invited to attend the first religious synod ever called in New England, and all ministers were asked to participate.

On August 3, Vane left with Lord Ley for England. Though he later distinguished himself as a defender of tolerance and as an eminent statesman, his efforts in Massachusetts had been un-

Thomas Hutchinson, Anne's great-great-grandson, was the 18th governor of Massachusetts. Rather unpopular with his constituents, he is highly regarded for his 1765 multivolume work, The History of the Colony and Province of Massachusetts-Bay, *to which he appended a transcript of his ancestor's trial.*

successful. Anne and her followers had no political voice left, and soon their chosen patron in doctrinal disputes would abandon them. Cotton had always been reluctant to speak directly with Anne and the Hutchinsonians, preferring the quiet of his study. He considered abandoning the chaotic Boston church at this point, but the rest of the ministers were aghast at driving so eminent a theologian away. The clergymen and numerous other interested parties streaming into Boston for the synod determined to bring Cotton over to their side, isolating Anne and Wheel-

wright. They spent three weeks conferring and preparing for the synod, which began on August 30 and continued for the next nine days. The discussions were as involved and arcane as ever, and the mood was conservative. Finally the body came up with 82 "opinions, some blasphemous, others erroneous, and all unsafe" plus 9 "unwholesome expressions" to condemn. When Anne's supporters demanded to know exactly who was accused of holding these views, so that they could defend themselves against a blanket denunciation, the synod refused to name the accused. Winthrop threatened the questioners with civil penalties if they persisted, and most of the Boston congregation stormed out in disgust. Cotton managed to reconcile his opinions with the rest of the clergy, but Wheelwright stubbornly refused to agree with three of their theological points. The synod ended with a condemnation of Anne and her clamorous adherents, as triumphantly recorded in Winthrop's journal:

1. That though women might meet (some few together) to pray and edify one another; yet such a set assembly, (as was then in practice at Boston,) where sixty or more did meet every week, and one woman (in a prophetical way, by resolving questions of doctrine, and expounding scripture) took upon her the whole exercise, was agreed to be disorderly, and without rule.

2. Though a private member might ask a question publicly after sermon for information; yet this ought to be

very wisely and sparingly done, and that with leave of the elders: but questions of reference . . . whereby the doctrines delivered were reproved, and the elders reproached, and that with bitterness, etc., was utterly condemned.

The General Court elected in May had repeatedly delayed judgment of Wheelwright. Armed with the pronouncements of the synod, Winthrop determined to put an end to factions in the colony. He needed a court wholly in agreement with him to carry out his plan. New elections were called, and another court convened, composed of members even more closely allied with Winthrop.

Although Vane had returned to England in early August, Wheelwright awaited sentencing, and Cotton had pulled away from her, she refused to back down. Directly across the street from Winthrop, she continued to deliver babies and nurse sick neighbors with her herbal medicines. Although she was nearing menopause (the point in a woman's life when her body can no longer bear children) she became pregnant one last time. Undeterred, she kept holding the crowded assemblies, attended by up to 80 people, that the synod had ruled illegal. She stayed busy until the day she left her house, on foot, for the November General Court, where she would be tried for disrupting the peace of Boston.

Hutchinson arrived in court on a gray, bitterly cold day. Winthrop wasted no time purging the court of any opposition. He used the petition

protesting the March verdict on Wheelwright to identify and root out Anne's and Wheelwright's supporters. Boston had sent three deputies: William Coddington, William Aspinwall, and John Coggeshall. Coddington was too prominent and too wealthy to attack, but the other two were found to have signed or approved of the petition, and they were summarily dismissed from their seats. William Colburn and John Oliver were elected as their replacements, but Oliver was dismissed for the same reason as Aspinwall and Coggeshall. Disgusted by the farcical proceedings, Bostonians refused to name another third deputy.

According to Winthrop and his hand-picked court, anyone who signed the appeal protesting Wheelwright's censure was not only unfit to serve on the court but also liable to prosecution himself. The governor's stratagem ensured Wheelwright's fate. No supporter of Wheelwright could judge him, but any opponent could. Wheelwright came before the court on November 2, 1637, and challenged the court to demonstrate precisely where in his fast day sermon he had slandered the ministers and magistrates and where he had promoted sedition. Their answers failed to satisfy him. A bitter dispute ensued, as Wheelwright maintained his innocence and the court accused him of encouraging almost every trouble during the preceding months. At last the magistrates and deputies found him guilty of stirring up the civil peace, of holding treacherous opinions, and of insulting behavior. He was disfranchised and banished from the colony. At first, he threatened again to appeal the case to the king, but Winthrop maintained that under the Massachusetts charter, the colony had the right to hear and determine all cases locally. Incensed, Wheelwright refused to remain under house arrest in Boston during the coming winter. He told them he would leave within 14 days.

Winthrop, who had been looking forward to this moment for a long time, called Anne Marbury Hutchinson before the court. She could not be accused of signing the petition or taking any other concrete political action, but the clergy who advised the court did their best to accuse her of numerous doctrinal errors. But to Winthrop's displeasure and to the surprise of several members of the General Court, for the remainder of the day and well into dusk, Anne defended her actions clearly and forcefully. Six ministers, beginning with Hugh Peter, were called and testified about her statements at Cotton's house a year earlier—claiming that she said they were not able ministers and taught a covenant of works. Forced by the late hour to adjourn the court, Winthrop admonished Anne to "consider of" all that had been said and be ready to proceed the next day.

Back in court the following morning Winthrop resumed proceedings. He announced that yesterday's hearing had provided "sufficient proof" of Anne's guilt. She wholeheartedly disagreed. Overnight, she had checked some notes from the December 1636 meeting and found differences between them and the ministers' testimony. She demanded that they repeat their testimony under oath, claiming, "An oath Sir is an end of all strife and it is God's ordinance."

Such an insult to the clergy angered them, and a heated discussion ensued. Winthrop claimed it was the court's decision whether there would be any oaths or not. Several ministers then spoke up. They worried that if they made a mistake under oath they would sin and might take God's name in vain. Others did not see the necessity of an oath because they deemed ministers implicitly trustworthy. Back and forth they argued until Winthrop demanded to know if there was anyone in the court who was not satisfied with the testimony of the ministers as already given.

To his surprise many responded, "We are not satisfied." A few stood up and urged that the ministers be put under oath. At last the ministers appeared ready to assent, but Winthrop would not relent. Instead he demanded that Anne produce witnesses to support her version of the conversation at Cotton's house. She called three men: John Coggeshall, Thomas Leverett, and John Cotton.

John Coggeshall, Anne's friend and neighbor, who had been stripped of his office as deputy for Boston for supporting Anne and the petition, courageously claimed, "Yes, I dare say that she did not say all that which they lay against her." The Reverend Hugh Peter lost control of his temper and shouted,

The Reverend Hugh Peter was the minister of Salem, Massachusetts, and one of Anne's most ferocious opponents. He returned to England in 1641 as an agent of the colony and distinguished himself in the English civil war against the forces of the king. When Charles I's son Charles II was restored to the English throne, Peter was disemboweled and hanged in public at Charing Cross, London, in 1660.

"How dare you look into Court and say such a word!" Stunned by Peter's vehement intolerance and complete scorn for legal procedure, Coggeshall subsided into silence. Thomas Leverett said that at the meeting Anne had merely said other ministers did not preach a covenant of grace as clearly as Cotton. His testimony corroborated Anne's, but the ministers disregarded his rather ineffectual assertion.

Reverend Cotton, her last witness, came over and sat down next to her. With the eloquence and brilliance that made him such an esteemed preacher, he glossed over Anne's differences with the conservative clergy. Pressed by Winthrop and Peter, Cotton maintained his composure as Peter fired question after question at him in an attempt to trip him up. At last he seemed to have soothed them. When Dudley demanded that Cotton tell them clearly whether or not "Mrs. Hutchinson did say they were not able ministers," Cotton finally replied he did not remember Anne saying that. The prosecution (who were also the witnesses) appeared defeated.

But Anne was exasperated with the proceedings. These ministers wran-

An illustration depicts banished colonists leaving Massachusetts. Wheelwright was banished from Boston and left during the winter of 1637; Anne was permitted to remain in the colony under house arrest until spring. Groups of supporters joined both leaders in their exile. Wheelwright led a party to Exeter in present-day New Hampshire.

gling over obscure expressions, Cotton's careful compromises—all seemed alien to her own understanding of her faith. The core of her disagreement with the established ministry was her rejection of narrow, legalistic thinking. She had always stressed the immediate knowledge of the Holy Spirit within a believer. In the end, she could not let her defense rest without stating her beliefs. She began a heartfelt speech that proved to be her undoing.

She began: "I shall give you the ground of what I know to be true. . . . I bless the Lord, he hath let me see which was the clear ministry and which the wrong. . . . Now if you do condemn me for speaking what in my conscience I know to be truth I must commit myself unto the Lord."

A member of the Court asked, "How do you know that that was the spirit?" (He implied that she might be mistaken about the Holy Spirit inspiring her.)

Hutchinson shot back with a reference to the Old Testament of the Bible: "How did Abraham know that it was God that bid him offer his son?"

Dudley responded, "By an immediate voice."

Hutchinson replied, "So to me by an immediate revelation."

Anne's assertion that she had received a revelation directly from God just as the ancient prophets had was a statement entirely against all Puritan doctrine. Dudley was astonished. He and the court were more incredulous still after Anne's next outburst.

Anne proclaimed her revelation had come to her "by the voice of his [God's] own spirit to my soul." She explained how carefully she had thought about which preachers taught the truth in England, how she "was then much troubled concerning the ministry under which I lived," and how she had followed Cotton to New England only to find the other ministers there as wrongheaded as those in England. Goaded beyond discretion by the injustice of the trial, she exploded, "You have power over my body but the Lord Jesus hath power over my body and soul, and assure yourselves this much . . . if you go on in this course . . . you will bring a curse upon you and your posterity, and the mouth of the Lord hath spoken it."

Israel Stoughton turned his back in horror at her curse. The court erupted as her enemies rushed over one another to add evidence of her blasphemy. William Bartholomew broke in to repeat what Anne had said about revelations in St. Paul's churchyard before she embarked for Massachusetts. Zechariah Symmes brought up her behavior on the voyage over the Atlantic. Cotton tried to soothe the enraged clergy without success. One minister denounced her "devilish delusion." Minor disputes and squabbles slowed the proceedings, but Anne's outburst sealed her fate. The court, led by Endecott, even began to attack Cotton until Winthrop reminded them that Anne alone was on trial. Winthrop prodded the court to vote for censure and banishment, blaming Anne's revelations for all of Boston's "disturbances" and calling her "the root of all the mischief."

Only two members of the court dissented. William Coddington, the sole deputy among Boston's original selections remaining on the court and Anne's staunch supporter, at last spoke up when he realized the court was about to vote to censure her. He noted: "You know it is a rule of the court that no man may be a judge and an accuser too. . . . I do not for my own part see any equity in the court in all your proceedings. Here is no law of God that she hath broken nor any law of the country that she hath broke. . . . She spake nothing to them [the accusing ministers] but in private . . . secret things ought to be spoken in secret and publick things in publick, therefore I think they have broken the rules of God's word."

Coddington's brave speech was to no avail. Dudley's response was a petulant complaint of hunger. Colburn, emboldened by his fellow deputy from Boston, flatly stated, "I dissent from censure of banishment." Winthrop heard no other voice speak up for Anne. The Reverends Thomas Weld and John Eliot perfunctorily testified under oath that they had indeed heard Anne disparage ministers at Cotton's house.

In triumph, Winthrop concluded the proceedings.

> The court hath already declared themselves satisfied concerning the things you hear, and concerning the troublesom[e]ness of her spirit and the danger of her course amongst us, which is not to be suffered. Therefore if it be the mind of the court that Mrs. Hutchinson for these things that appear before us is unfit for our society, and if it be the mind of the court that she shall be banished out of our liberties and imprisoned till she be sent away, let them hold up their hands.

All but three raised their hand. Coddington and Colburn voted in opposition, and a Mr. Jennison abstained. Winthrop continued.

> WINTHROP: Mrs. Hutchinson, the sentence of the court you hear is that you are banished from out of our jurisdiction as being a woman not fit for our society, and are to be imprisoned till the court shall send you away.
> HUTCHINSON: I desire to know wherefore I am banished.
> WINTHROP: Say no more, the court knows wherefore and is satisfied.

93

A sculpture of Anne Hutchinson and one of her daughters stands outside the Massachusetts State House. Winthrop and such later Puritan writers as Cotton Mather reviled her after her death, but succeeding generations saw her as a courageous fighter in the struggle for religious liberty.

EIGHT

"Rather a Preacher than a Hearer"

The General Court passed sentence on Anne on November 8, 1637. Exhausted from the tumultuous proceedings, the court recessed for one week and met again on Wednesday, November 15. Using the March 1636 petition on behalf of Wheelwright as a guide, Winthrop moved quickly to identify and to crush Anne's remaining support. The court called two members of the honor guard who had refused to attend Winthrop and disenfranchised them: Edward Hutchinson, a brother-in-law of Anne's, and William Balston, an innkeeper. Neither man submitted meekly. Hutchinson protested his heavy fine of 40 pounds and was tossed in jail for a night. Balston pointed out, "If such a petition had been made in any other place in the world there would have been no fault found with it." But the petition had been made in Massachusetts Bay Colony, and the magistrates and ministers could not tolerate any challenge to their author-

ity. Carefully checking off names from the signatures appended to the petition, the court stripped several more freemen, including well-established merchants, of citizenship during the next three days. Among them were Thomas Marshall, the town ferryman who had known Anne in Alford and esteemed her in Boston; William Dinely, the barber-surgeon who worked with Anne among the sick; William Dyer, whose wife, Mary, was devoted to Anne, especially after Anne's care helped her live through a terrible pregnancy and stillbirth; Richard Gridley, a brickmaker; and Captain John Underhill, who had fought in the Pequot War. Finally, the court moved that the college which was to have been established in Boston be established in Newtown instead, for that town had been kept free from the opinions of Anne Hutchinson. The college was later named Harvard.

The General Court decided that grave as Anne's case was, they could not in good conscience banish a pregnant, middle-aged woman during the harsh New England winter. While the court proceeded with its judgments against her friends, Anne was allowed to return to Boston to gather a few personal belongings and arrange for the care of her family—she still had 7 children ranging in age from 10 to 1 living at home—before she made the treacherous 2-mile trip over Boston Neck to Roxbury, where she would be imprisoned at her husband's expense. She remained under guard at the home of Joseph Weld, brother of the Reverend Thomas Weld (one of her prosecutors), far from her friends and family.

Trials of Anne's supporters ended on Friday, November 17. The following Monday, Winthrop boldly returned to the attack. The General Court ordered every freeman who signed the Wheelwright petition either to surrender his guns, powder, and ammunition or to acknowledge his sin in signing the document and recant. The court order was read to 58 Boston freemen, 5 men of Salem, 5 from Roxbury, 3 from Newbury, and 2 each from Ipswich and Charlestown. At the home of Captain Robert Keayne, 75 men were disarmed. Within a few days, 30 men reversed themselves, apologized for signing the petition, and received their arms back. Five more claimed their name had been forged and they were not guilty. Still, despite the nearly overwhelming pressure from the court, 40 men refused to give in and to rebuke Anne.

All of Winthrop's efforts could not stamp out Anne's supporters entirely.

Several of her staunchest followers determined to rebuke their governor in church for his actions at the General Court. They approached Cotton and Wilson, but unsurprisingly, Wilson was not eager to admonish the governor, who helped him subdue the woman who had nearly toppled him from his post as preacher at the First Church of Boston. Somehow Winthrop caught wind of the group's attempt and rose during one Sunday service to address the congregation. As he noted in his journal, "Understanding their intent, [I] thought fit to prevent such a public disorder, and so took occasion to speak to the congregation to this effect." He claimed that the church could criticize the actions of an elected official in his private life but had no right to admonish him for the performance of his civic duties. He nevertheless asserted that it was "most for the glory of God, and the public good, to pass sentence as [we] did." Ironically, Winthrop saw nothing wrong with the General Court's enforcing civic penalties on Anne and the Hutchinsonians for their religious activities, though he denied the church could admonish congregants for governmental proceedings.

Around this time, Cotton began to talk of leaving Boston for a newly founded colony at New Haven. He felt Anne and her followers had taken advantage of him, claiming that their ideas were his own. He concluded that they had misunderstood the delicate and complicated nuances of his thought and pushed his emphasis on a covenant of grace to heretical extremes.

An interior view of a typical Puritan home suggests the conditions in which Anne spent the winter after her trial. She remained under house arrest in the home of Joseph Weld, brother of one of her fierce opponents, the Reverend Thomas Weld. Only her family and those ministers who tried to sway her to their side were allowed to visit.

In addition, he did not like the alien exclusion law, for it allowed no new people to settle in the colony, and as a consequence no new congregants were joining the church. When Winthrop heard that Cotton might depart, he wasted no time in persuading the esteemed theologian to stay. Winthrop knew that if news of Cotton's desertion reached England, the colony's reputation would be irreparably damaged.

Everyone in the Massachusetts Bay Colony suffered through the worst winter in years. Consequently, Anne saw little of her family and friends, but a constant procession of ministers made their way to Roxbury to urge her to see their light. Enduring the progress of her last pregnancy and the approach of menopause, Anne spent a difficult winter. She had seen other women experience these physical changes, and her knowledge helped relieve her of some anxiety. As always, she sought comfort in closely reading the Bible.

Anne spent four months in Weld's house, cut off from Boston. There, and in several outer settlements as well, the ministers labored to cleanse their church of any Hutchinsonian taint.

Weld expelled three of Anne's supporters from his church at Roxbury. Cotton, "finding how he had been abused . . . did spend most of his time, both publicly and privately, to discover . . . errors, and to reduce such as were gone astray," as Winthrop noted. The magistrates eagerly consulted with ministers to identify and criticize Anne's ideas. Any doctrine they disliked that Anne might possibly have held was examined and denounced from the pulpit. Some preachers even claimed she had come up with newly blasphemous tenets during her confinement at Roxbury and continued to infect their parishioners' thoughts. Anne found the news that the ministers were busily gathering what they called "the growing evils" of her secret opinions disheartening. Sequestered in a house far from Boston, separated from her disciples by miles of frozen mud paths, prevented from seeing all but her family and hectoring ministers, she was still accused of supplying subversive opinions.

She consoled herself by reading the Bible and took comfort from the visits of her husband, William. Throughout her long judicial ordeal, William had been by her side. A quiet, stable, hardworking man, he was not one to hurl himself into public disputes. Few records of his words exist, but his behavior was that of a devoted husband. During that long, icy winter, Anne and William discussed their future home, which would be far outside the boundaries of the Massachusetts Bay Colony and free from the strictures of its mag-

istrates and ministers. They waited for spring, when Anne had to leave the colony by order of the court and they would be able to start afresh.

But William could not always be with her at Weld's house, for he had to attend to his textile business and their family. Anne had nothing else to occupy her time—no neighbors to take care of and chat with, no children to teach, no household to manage. For an energetic woman, such idleness was painful. When the Reverends Weld, Eliot, and Shephard came to discuss religion with her, she eagerly spoke about perplexing verses of the Bible and her own understanding of how Puritan beliefs resolved the dilemmas posed by conflicting scriptural passages. Trained long ago in religious studies by her father in England, she welcomed the opportunity to examine and resolve doctrinal questions. Her clerical visitors viewed the conversations in a very different light.

By March 1638, they had collected 29 of what they termed her "gross errors." She was summoned to the First Church of Boston on Thursday, March 15, to answer charges. The penalty of banishment by the secular authorities had not satisfied the wounded pride of the colony's ministers. They determined to deal with her "in a Church way," or to expel her from the church as well as the colony.

Throughout the preceding January and February, William Coddington had struggled with his conscience. Although he had spoken his mind forcefully at Anne's trial before the General

Court, he remained deeply troubled by the injustice of the proceedings, which in the end were not a trial at all, for the judges were the prosecutors and had determined their verdict long before Anne defended herself. One of the richest men in the colony, he decided he could no longer live under such repression and gathered a group of men to start a settlement outside the colony's borders. William Hutchinson, bound by ties of affection to Anne, had to leave, along with those of her supporters who had been banished, but other members of this group freely chose to leave. On February 19, Coggeshall and Aspinwall wrote to another religious leader expelled from Massachusetts, Roger Williams, to ask if land was available in Rhode Island. His answer was positive, and less than one month later, on March 7, 19 men met in the well-furnished parlor of Coddington's house—the first brick house built in Boston—and signed an agreement to govern themselves and settle in Rhode Island. Among them were Coggeshall, Aspinwall, William Hutchinson and his son Edward, and his brother, Edward, Sr., William Dyer, William Balston, and a dozen more ardent supporters of Anne's.

William and a few others left immediately to scout out good locations for their settlement. A little more than a week later, Anne journeyed to the First Church of Boston. She was late and arrived after the usual Thursday two-hour lecture. Her friend the surgeon Thomas Oliver was by then a ruling elder of the church; he convinced the ministers that Anne was not showing contempt for them but instead had been late for medical reasons: She was pregnant and weak.

Wan and drawn, Anne returned to a town that held very few still faithful to her. Her closest allies were in Rhode Island, and those who had been victims of Winthrop's decrees feared any further connection with her. This hearing was even more dismal for Anne than her trial. The ministers with whom she had discussed religion during the long winter repeated her questions and musings as if they were long-held blasphemous doctrines. For nearly nine hours, they berated her and questioned her. One called her a dangerous woman who spread her corrupt opinions like a disease. Even Cotton rose to admonish her. When her son Edward and son-in-law Thomas Savage rose to protest that Anne was being misunderstood, they were admonished as well.

Cotton turned to them, accusing the two of encouraging Anne to continue in evil ways. He then told the women there that he thought Anne had led them gravely astray. Addressing Anne, he stated: "You have been an instrument of doing some good amongst us . . . [but] these unsound tenets of yours . . . and the evil of your opinions do outweigh all the good of your doings." He went on, "She is but a woman, and many unsound and dangerous principles are held by her." Seeing Anne dispirited, depressed, and exhausted by their abuse, the court sent her to stay with Cotton for a week. Perhaps Cotton took some pity on his long-ago admirer and hoped he could convince her that she had been wrong to challenge the established ministry.

When the proceedings reconvened on March 22, Anne had not given up. She attempted to apologize and admitted she had expressed herself "rashly and unadvisedly" in November. She said it had not been her intention to slight the ministers, the Scriptures, or the church. Nothing she could say would satisfy the assembled clergy. Wilson led a vicious attack and unleashed a torrent of abuse from Eliot, Shephard, and especially Peter, who stormed, "You have rather been a husband than a wife, a preacher than a hearer, and a magistrate than a subject, . . . and have not been humbled for this." Wilson called her a "dangerous instrument of the Devil, raised up by Satan amongst us." Cotton balked at actually expelling Anne himself and at his request, Wilson gleefully took on the job. He stood and addressed Anne:

> The Church consenting to it we will proceed to excommunication. . . . Forasmuch as you, Mrs. Hutchinson, have highly transgressed and offended . . . and troubled the Church with your Errors. . . . I do cast you out . . . and deliver you up to Satan. . . . I command you in the name of Christ Jesus and of this Church as a Leper to withdraw yourselfe out of the Congregation.

Anne's battle ended at last. Head held high, she marched down the aisle of the meetinghouse. Mary Dyer left her seat, slipped her arm through Anne's, and accompanied her out. As they left, someone by the door said, "The Lord sanctify this unto you." (The remark implied that the Lord would show Anne the court's verdict was correct.) Anne replied: "The Lord judgeth not as man judgeth. Better to be cast out of the Church than to deny Christ."

Almost 47 years old and quite pregnant, Anne was given less than a week to prepare to leave Massachusetts with her children and what belongings she could transport. On March 28 she left to join her husband, who, along with Coddington and others, had settled on the island of Aquidneck, near the present-day site of Newport, Rhode Island.

Aquidneck lay about 65 miles south of Boston. For almost a week, Anne and the small party accompanying her slogged through muddy trails, canoed across rivers and streams swollen with melted snow, and braved the perils of attack by unfriendly Native Americans or robbers. Coddington, who had been chosen governor of the new settlement, later wrote to Winthrop of his journey, "What myself and wife and family did endure in that removal, I wish neither you nor yours may ever be put unto." Occasionally, they found an abandoned hut in which they could huddle at night for some protection. Finally, Hutchinson was reunited with her husband and set to work furnishing the primitive cabin that would be their home.

The strain of the last several months and the grueling journey weakened Anne, who fell sick. In July, six weeks before her due date and twisted with pain, she sent for the local preacher,

John Clarke. Like Anne and William Hutchinson, he feared the worst. Anne survived, but she did suffer a painful, bloody miscarriage. Her last pregnancy ended horribly, but when Winthrop, who had been keeping alert for news of her, heard of the tragedy he was delighted. He claimed that the stillbirth was God's punishment for her sins—that her evil ways made her "bring forth deformed monsters." Weld spread the rumor that Anne had delivered "thirty monstrous births" and called her new home the "Island of Errors."

But Anne, who to Winthrop's dismay "revived again, and . . . gloried in her sufferings" after her excommunication, was an uncommonly strong woman. In Aquidneck, freed from the persecution of the ministers of Massachusetts Bay Colony, she regained her physical strength and welcomed many of her followers, who emigrated to Aquidneck to join her.

Within a year of her excommunication, Anne took up preaching in her new home. Winthrop found her strength, courage, and integrity infuriating. When he learned she and Roger Williams were thriving, he was incredulous. He lamented in his journal: "At Providence things grew still worse. . . . At Aquiday [Aquidneck], also, Mrs Hutchinson exercised publicly." When she sent a letter to the First Church of Boston, the elders refused to read it, and Winthrop sighed with relief, glad that excommunication meant no communication whatsoever. Nevertheless, the little colony at Aquidneck attracted more immigrants.

In the spring of 1639, William Hutchinson replaced Coddington as governor of the growing community. In 1640, the General Court, under Winthrop's direction, sent a party of three to Anne in another attempt to "reduce" her. She refused to listen to them. They approached her husband hoping to draw him away from his wife's teachings, but he told them that "he was more nearly tied to his wife than to the church; he thought her to be a dear saint and servant of God." A son of Thomas Oliver, one of the three envoys, reported: "We told her, we had a message to her from the church of Christ in Boston. . . . She would not acknowledge it any church of Christ."

By 1641, Hutchinson's following had grown even larger. Winthrop could not assuage his continuing anger at her success. When her son Francis and son-in-law William Collins visited Boston, Winthrop summoned them to appear before the General Court, probably to abuse and denounce them. They declined to do so, and Winthrop fined them heavily. They refused to pay, and Winthrop jailed the two. The expense of their imprisonment proved too much for the colony, and they were freed without paying a cent. Winthrop had failed again to punish Anne from afar. Enraged, he banished the young men from Boston and threatened them with execution should they ever return.

Four years of struggle in the wilderness and relentless but impotent attacks from Winthrop could not daunt Anne's spirit, but personal tragedy took a heavy toll. In 1642, William Hutchin-

Anne, six of her children, and a few companions moved to Dutch territory in present-day New York State in 1642. Native Americans went to war with the Dutch the following spring, attacking boats on the Hudson River and plundering plantations. In the fall, a band of warriors massacred Anne and all but one of her children.

son died. He had been not only Anne's husband but also her closest friend and lifelong partner. Deeply grieved, Anne decided to leave Aquidneck for a small community near present-day Pelham Bay, New York. Talk of union with the Massachusetts Bay Colony filled the air, and Anne could not bear to face the vituperation of Winthrop and the clergy again without her beloved William. Her destination was part of a colony owned by the Dutch, and the authorities of Massachusetts had no power to harm her there. Six of her children, her son-in-law William Collins, and several other families went with her. Her small house was built on an isolated site called Anne's Hoeck (point), between a river (the present-day Hutchinson River) and a small rise in the land.

A year later, sometime in the late summer or early fall of 1643, tragedy struck again. A local war between the Dutch and the Native Americans broke out, and Anne's party was caught amid the fighting. Native Americans massacred her and five of her children. Only 10-year-old Susanna was spared, and fortunately friends of the family in Boston ransomed the young girl a few years later.

Anne's fame and influence did not die with her. Soon after her death, Winthrop wrote an account of the controversy she caused in Boston. Published under Weld's name, it was titled *A Short Story of the Rise, Reign, and Ruin of the Antinomians, and Libertines that Infected the Churches of New England.* Winthrop's bias is clear, and he described Anne's behavior with virulent hatred. The pamphlet was written specifically to be read in England and to present the activities of Winthrop's government in the best possible light. Winthrop feared Anne even after her death.

Most of Anne's enemies were sure they were finally free of their affliction. But in England, where a civil war was waging, the Puritans were splitting into two groups: those who espoused ideas similar to Anne's—the Presbyterians—and those who endorsed the ideas of the First Church of Boston—the Congregationalists. In New England, many of Hutchinson's followers became members of the Society of Friends, commonly called Quakers. Quakers had no church hierarchy at all and believed in an inner light that guided one's actions, much as Anne had stressed a believer's knowledge of the Holy Spirit within one. Coddington, who had moved to Aquidneck with her and then to New York, became a Quaker in 1656. Hutchinson's sister Katherine joined the Society of Friends and was whipped and imprisoned for preaching.

The new religion became so popular that in 1658 the General Court of Massachusetts Bay Colony voted to banish or hang any Quakers in the colony. Hutchinson's old friend, Mary Dyer, defied the new law and was sentenced to prison twice. When she persisted in her refusal to leave or reject Quakerism, she was hanged in Boston on June 1, 1660.

Not until 1676 did the first account supporting Anne and her ideas appear.

The Native American who killed Anne took the name of her settlement as his own—Anne's Hoeck. His signature is preserved by the Eastchester Historical Society.

An 1869 painting depicts Mary Dyer being led to her hanging in Boston in 1660; she was punished for refusing to abandon Quakerism or depart from the colony. Although Anne did not establish a new denomination herself, a number of her followers, including William Coddington, joined the Society of Friends. Quakers were persecuted by Boston authorities even more harshly than Anne and her followers had been.

The anonymous pamphlet was titled *A Glass for the People of New England, in Which They May See Themselves and Spirits, and If not Too Late, Repent and Turn from Their Abominable Ways and Cursed Contrivances.* Several more texts appeared, based on Winthrop's journals, which he kept before, during, and after Anne's time in Boston. Finally, in 1765, Anne's prominent great-great-grandson Thomas Hutchinson (who served as lieutenant governor and governor of the colony) wrote *The History of the Colony and Province of Massachusetts-Bay.* He appended to his multivolume account a transcription of Anne's trial written by an anonymous, sympathetic listener. His book offered its readers a far more balanced view of the trial than Winthrop's *Short Story* did. Later, in the 19th century, several historians recognized Anne's struggle as one of the earliest battles against religious intolerance in American history.

Anne Hutchinson failed to revolutionize the structure of church and state in Massachusetts, but Winthrop's efforts as governor of the Massachusetts Bay Colony and Wilson's efforts as pastor of the First Church of Boston failed to silence her. In fact, they assured her a place in history when they allowed her to speak at her trial and excommunication. Both records clearly show her strength, intelligence, and tenacity. Governmental and religious sanctions could not crush her indomitable spirit, and her lack of political power did not prevent her from shaking the foundations of the colony. In Boston she drew a tremendous following that included some of the most prominent merchants of the day; in Rhode Island she attracted scores of adherents repelled by the repressive conformity of the Massachusetts Bay Colony. She was, as she had said of the Woman of Ely, "A woman of a thousand, hardly any like her."

FURTHER READING

Adams, Charles Francis. *Three Episodes of Massachusetts History: The Settlement of Boston Bay; The Antinomian Controversy; A Study of Church and Town Government.* 2 vols. 1892. Reprint. New York: Russell and Russell, 1965.

Battis, Emery John. *Saints and Sectaries: Anne Hutchinson and the Antinomian Controversy in the Massachusetts Bay Colony.* Chapel Hill: University of North Carolina Press, 1962.

Holliday, Carl. *Woman's Life in Colonial Days.* Detroit: Gale Research Company, 1970.

Hutchinson, Thomas. *The History of the Colony and Province of Massachusetts Bay.* Vol. 2. Edited by Lawrence Shaw Mayo. Cambridge: Harvard University Press, 1936.

Williams, Selma R. *Divine Rebel: The Life of Anne Marbury Hutchinson.* New York: Holt, Rinehart & Winston, 1981.

Winthrop, John. *Winthrop's Journal, History of New England: 1630–1649.* Vol. 1. 1908. Reprint. Edited by James Kendall Hosmer. New York: Barnes & Noble, 1959.

CHRONOLOGY

ca. July 17, 1591	Born Anne Marbury in Alford, Lincolnshire, England
1605	Father, Francis Marbury, is appointed minister at the church of St. Martin's in the Vintry; Anne moves with her family to London
1611	Francis Marbury dies
1612	Anne marries William Hutchinson; they move to Alford
1613	Anne gives birth to Edward, the first of her 15 children
ca. 1614	Becomes an ardent follower of the Reverend John Cotton, minister at Boston, Lincolnshire
1630	Two of Anne's children die within a month; Anne experiences a crisis of faith
1633	The Reverend John Cotton flees from England and sails to the Massachusetts Bay Colony; the Hutchinsons consider emigrating to the colony
1634	Anne sails for the Massachusetts Bay Colony in New England with William and their 11 children
1635	Begins holding assemblies for women in her home
1636	Anne's views become more controversial as they diverge from the established orthodox doctrine; her criticisms of several ministers attract wide support among prominent Bostonians; former governor John Winthrop and the Reverend John Wilson oppose her faction
1637	John Winthrop elected governor; Anne is brought to trial by secular authorities for inciting religious disharmony and stirring up political dissent; the General Court sentences her to banishment
1638	Anne is cast out of the church by ministers of the First Church of Boston; leaves Massachusetts to join her husband on the island of Aquidneck in Rhode Island; suffers a painful miscarriage
1639	Begins preaching in Aquidneck
1642	William Hutchinson dies; Anne leaves Aquidneck for a settlement in Dutch territory near present-day Pelham Bay, New York
1643	Anne and five of her children are killed by Native Americans at war with the Dutch

INDEX

PICTURE CREDITS

Bettmann Archive: frontispiece, pp. 12, 18, 20, 22–23, 25, 26, 29, 36, 39, 41, 44, 45, 46, 49, 55, 58, 59, 63, 64, 102; Culver Pictures: pp. 16, 48, 56, 80, 86, 90–91, 97; Eastchester Historical Society: p. 103; Courtesy Essex Institute Library, Salem, MA, photo by Richard Merrill: p. 61; Library of Congress: pp. 30–31, 33, 51, 54, 68, 71, 72, 76–77, 89, 94; Massachusetts Historical Society: p. 73; Massachusetts State Archives: p. 66; The New-York Historical Society: pp. 53, 84, 104; The New York Public Library Picture Collection: p. 34; Courtesy of the Rhode Island Historical Society: p. 70

Elizabeth IlgenFritz graduated from Sarah Lawrence College with a B.A. in literature and American history. She is a writer who lives in Westchester County, New York, where she is at work on a collection of short stories.

❖   ❖   ❖

Matina S. Horner is president emerita of Radcliffe College and associate professor of psychology and social relations at Harvard University. She is best known for her studies of women's motivation, achievement, and personality development. Dr. Horner serves on several national boards and advisory councils, including those of the National Science Foundation, Time Inc., and the Women's Research and Education Institute. She earned her B.A. from Bryn Mawr College and Ph.D. from the University of Michigan, and holds honorary degrees from many colleges and universities, including Mount Holyoke, Smith, Tufts, and the University of Pennsylvania.